D1430931

How to Avoid Alienating Your Kids in 10 Easy Steps

How to Avoid Alienating Your Kids in 10 Easy Steps

GREG CYNAUMON, Ph.D.,
with DANA CYNAUMON

MOODY PRESS
CHICAGO

© 1993 by
GREG CYNAUMON

All rights reserved. No part of this book may be reproduced in any form without permission in writing from the publisher, except in the case of brief quotations embodied in critical articles or reviews.

All Scripture quotations, unless indicated, are taken from the *Holy Bible: New International Version*®. NIV®. Copyright © 1973, 1978, 1984, International Bible Society. Used by permission of Zondervan Publishing House. All rights reserved.

Scripture quotations marked (NASB) are taken from the *New American Standard Bible*, © 1960, 1962, 1963, 1968, 1971, 1972, 1973, 1975, and 1977 by The Lockman Foundation, and are used by permission.

The use of selected references from various versions of the Bible in this publication does not necessarily imply publisher endorsement of the versions in their entirety.

ISBN: 0-8024-8576-6

1 3 5 7 9 10 8 6 4 2

Printed in the United States of America

To Jan, my beautiful wife of thirteen years. A woman of unswerving support and unparalleled patience. I've needed the support, and you've shown me the patience. Not exactly an even trade, but thanks anyway. You are the very essence of grace.

And to my kids, Tracy and Matt, who have made fatherhood the greatest experience on earth. Please don't ruin it when you become teenagers.

As for my co-writer and partner, Dana, it's a good thing we're brothers, otherwise I'd be all alone with this warped sense of humor. I cherish our relationship. Thanks for sharing him with me for the past year, Pam.

To my parents, Ed and Myrna, I thank you for your love, support, and wonderful role modeling. (With the exception of our family camping trips.)

To my friends and colleagues at the American Psychological Institute in Anaheim Hills, California, I thank you for your support and encouragement.

This book is really dedicated to you—parents and future parents. Sit back, relax, and put your feet up. Parenting isn't as scary as it looks.

CONTENTS

INTRODUCTION

None of us sets out to deliberately alienate our kids. We don't suddenly wake up one morning, turn to our spouse, and say, "Honey, what do you say to starting a family so we can have a couple of kids to torment?" or, "Isn't it about time we began making our children just as miserable as we were growing up . . . maybe even more?"

The opposite, of course, is true. We welcome the birth of our children with all the pomp and painstaking preparation usually reserved for a presidential visit. Mom hangs wallpaper in the nursery—a task she enjoys about as much as getting a root canal. Dad patiently wades through hopelessly complicated instructions on how to assemble a crib—a job he would normally spring on an unsuspecting neighbor. We roll out the red carpet all right, only it's in the form of soft, quilted blankets and a veritable menagerie of stuffed animals. It's almost as if we are trying to make a good first impression with the new baby, and I suppose we are.

Finally, that fateful, wondrous day dawns. The baby arrives on time—give or take what seems like a millennium—and is beautiful. Dad emerges from the delivery room slightly disheveled but beaming as he passes out cheap cigars that nobody dares to smoke. And Mom? She's euphoric, exhausted, having already forgotten all those strange, new names she called her husband during the delivery.

A new family is born—Mom, Dad, and the baby. The three of you, just kind of staring at each other and wondering, "OK, what's next, and who's in charge here?"

Now would be an excellent time for my latest fantasy breakthrough—the "parenting patch," time-released wisdom and patience absorbed through the skin directly into the central nervous system, making parenthood a snap. You would automatically treat your kids with dignity, trust, and respect. You would always be consistently firm but fair. There would be no more yelling or threatening. And you would unfailingly find just the right words for any situation. If there were such a patch, you can be sure that our kids would hire a limo to whisk us straight to the pharmacy the minute the patch began wearing off.

Naturally, your kids would grow up perfect as well. They would be "hassle-free," honest, well-adjusted children who made straight A's and handled their screaming hormones without a hitch. They would volunteer to mow the lawn, wax your car, and get up early each Saturday to grind the beans for fresh coffee to go with your breakfast. Yeah, right.

Seriously, the birth of a child is an extraordinary opportunity! A chance to begin with a clean slate. Unfortunately, many of us forget to wipe down that slate in advance. We take our own childhood experiences and memories along for the ride.

We bring the warm memories of nurturing, well-balanced parents who lovingly guided us with precision through the trials of childhood, while endowing us with a positive sense of "self" and respect for others. Unfortunately, we also carry with us painful memories—vivid, nightmarish feelings of abandonment, minimization, rejection, or abuse that crippled our growth and devastated our self-esteem.

We bring it all—the good, the bad, and the ugly. The reality is we are only human, which makes us uniquely capable of "messing up." We mess up with our mates. We mess up with our bosses. We put colored clothes in the washer with whites—at least I do. And we mess up regularly when it comes to raising our kids.

As a family therapist, I often speak to groups of parents. I begin each talk with the following statement: "Nobody but nobody is an expert on your child, except you. For all of the well-meaning friends, authors, psychologists, and relatives who tell you how to be the perfect parent, not a single one of them knows your child like you do. Like fingerprints, no two children are the same—neither are any two parents."

No, we don't set out to deliberately alienate our kids. We all want to be good parents. But how many Bill Cosbys are there in parenting? Conversely, nobody is born with a recessive gene that dooms them to rearing children who habitually shave the kitty or chase the neighbor kids around the yard with the chain saw. No, none of us sets out to alienate our children.

The secret to successful parenting is to fully flesh out and understand at least ten of the most common ways we alienate our kids. Why ten? Psychological studies have shown that we are really only able to store, retain, and access ten major points pertaining to any one subject. Since libraries are full of pointers on parenting, it is impossible to expect parents to read and digest them all. So we've compiled only the most important points—handy parenting tools to assist you in reaching your parenting potential.

If you retain and implement these ten easy steps, I'm confident that you will not only become a more effective parent, but you will derive more enjoyment from the child-rearing experience—and your kids will enjoy you more, too. However, if you really insist on alienating your kids, read on—we'll show you how to do that as well.

1

If You Really Want to Alienate Your Kids . . .

DEVELOP A RIGID AND CONTROLLING PARENTING STYLE

The moment we received the good news from our home pregnancy kit (let's see, minus is no, plus is yes—what does an exclamation point mean, triplets?) we shifted into overdrive. We scurried about like a pair of hyper pack rats collecting and stashing enough baby food, cotton swabs, diaper wipes, and ear plugs (for me) to meet the demands of a small country for a month.

We had all our baby bottles in a row. We even spruced up the spare bedroom in anticipation of the season's second blessed arrival, my mother-in-law. Which reminds me—Adam had no mother-in-law. That's how we know he lived in paradise.

Just as we were about to "kick back," relax, and enjoy our first pregnancy (at least I was), somebody had the nerve to ask, "So what kind of parenting style are you guys going to use?"

"Style? Oh, we're just planning to be the best parents we can be," I said, trying to keep from sounding foolish. It was too late. So much for relaxation. For quite some time I struggled to put this "style" thing into perspective—and even longer trying to define it.

Let's begin with the premise that we all have our own parenting style, that is, our unique way of doing things. It then becomes helpful to identify those tendencies. Place them under a microscope. Discover how they work, don't work, and why. After you've compared, poked, and prodded these styles until you understand what makes them tick, you will probably notice a pattern emerging—one that reveals the "flash points" in your own parenting style, sticking spots that may be contributing to the alienation of your children. You won't like everything you see—nobody does—but you will be in a far better position to tap into the positive aspects and dispose of the bad.

The real trick is finding a parenting style that suits your personality—who you are. Any attempt to drastically alter or adapt your "core" parenting style to another would be like forcing a sumo wrestler to become an Olympic pole vaulter. You'd probably both fall on your face—or other parts of your anatomy. Don't worry, though, there's plenty of maneuvering room for improvement in most parenting styles.

Let's begin by visiting two of the most troublesome parenting styles and the trail of problems they can leave. Next, we'll introduce you to the star of our story—the balanced parent. Ultimately, though, it's up to you to integrate the characteristics of the balanced parent into your own style.

After observing and studying thousands of families over a fifteen-year span—first as a police officer (more about my police years later) and then as a therapist—I have concluded that there are essentially three main parenting styles. The first two can be disastrous; the third should be our ultimate destination as parents.

✔ **The rigid and controlling parent**
✔ **The overly permissive parent**
✔ **The well-balanced parent**

There are other troublesome tributaries that flow from these parenting categories, but the rigid and controlling parent is by far the most problematic, followed closely by the overly permissive parent. Our goal is to understand the pitfalls of both troublesome parenting styles and how to avoid them on our way to becoming well-balanced parents.

THE RIGID AND CONTROLLING PARENT

The single most effective way to alienate your kids is by being rigid and controlling. It works every time. Meet whom I affectionately call the platoon parent. These men and women are always on a mission, patrolling the house in camouflage Bermudas with a can of Lysol at the ready. They check for dilated pupils with penlight, have considered "hooking up" their kids to lie detectors, and favor stringing miles of barbed wire around the house to keep *their* kids in and *enemy* kids out. They are the commandants of their own prisoner-of-war camps, with more rules, regulations, and edicts than any kid could possibly obey.

How do seemingly normal people become platoon parents? They probably had good teachers when *they* were young—their parents. It's like being born into a family of dentists (painful thought). Your great-grandad was a dentist, your grandfather was a dentist, and your father was a dentist. The deck was stacked against you becoming anything else, despite the fact that fillings make you feel faint and flossing makes you gag. You even break into a cold sweat anytime you hear the words "OK . . . rinse."

Rigid and controlling parents often received little or no respect when they were kids. They were probably made to feel minimized, insecure, and less significant than everyone else, especially their parents. Why? Because these parents also came from homes that were ruled with an "iron fist."

TRAITS OF A "PLATOON PARENT"

Do any of these platoon parent statements sound familiar?

- ☐ "As long as you live under my roof, you'll do what I tell you to do!"
- ☐ "You're just a kid. Don't tell me how to run this house!"
- ☐ "Act your age!"

☐ "Grow up!"
☐ "What makes you think you have a say in what goes on around here?"
☐ "When you're eighteen, then you can do whatever you want. Until then . . ."
☐ "You make me sick. I don't even want to look at you right now!"
☐ "God and the Bible give me the authority to tell you what to do!"
☐ "The Bible says children must obey their parents!"
☐ "When I was your age, I never smarted-off to my parents!"
☐ "You better start showing me respect!"
☐ "Where did I go wrong?"
☐ "You think *you* have it bad around here . . . you should have seen *my* parents!"

Rigid and controlling parents come not only from angry or abusive homes but from homes without structure or discipline, homes void of consistent boundaries and limits, broken homes, homes where mother and infant failed to bond during critical stages of early development, homes with no discernable paths that force a child onto roads that vanish in a sandstorm of mixed messages.

Parents from these kinds of homes often overcompensate in a futile attempt to become the positive role model they never had. The problem is, if they never had a positive role model, how can they play the part? Did you ever try to give a book report in front of your fifth-grade class only to realize that you forgot to read the book? You improvised but ultimately failed—at least I did. Rigid and controlling parents are often heard to say, "My parents could've cared less what I did growing up. I'm not going to let you get away with the same things I did."

A Case Example of a Rigid and Controlling Parent

Ron reluctantly (angry and defensive) came into my office at the insistence of his wife, Becky, and their pastor. After eight, mostly unhappy, years of marriage, she had finally reached the limits of her patience. As I attempted to begin a dialogue, Ron sprang to his own defense.

"Let me tell you what the problem is before she jumps in and makes you think everything is my fault," he shouted, the veins bulging in his neck. Sucking in a long breath, he began his harangue. "I am sick and tired of Becky and my smart-mouthed, teenage daughter ganging up on me. Whenever I lay down the law, my sixteen-year-old goes to my wife, whining about how strict and unfair I am. So my wife caves in and tells her to go ahead and do whatever she wants. Well, I've had it! Let her hang out at the mall with her looser friends. Let her go to concerts with boys we don't even know, where there's undoubtedly drinking, drugs, and smoking going on. I'm fed up with this garbage of not getting any respect from my wife and smart-mouthed daughter, and it's going to stop!"

I turned my attention to Becky, who was sinking farther into the cushions of the couch with each angry syllable. "Is this the way you see the family situation as well, Becky?" I asked.

She looked downward for a moment and replied meekly, "I want to be a good, obedient wife and not be disagreeable, but Ron is driving our daughter away. He doesn't trust her to do anything without giving her the third degree. He is so strict that she has to lie about where she goes and who she's with. We are all so afraid of his anger that nobody dares say anything for fear he will explode."

"Well, then, why don't you just do what I ask?" Ron screamed, grabbing his faded windbreaker, before firing off another salvo. "I've told you time and again, and now you sit here and say, 'I guess I shouldn't go against his wishes.' You know what, Becky? I don't need help, you do!" He then leveled a parting shot in my direction, "So how much is it going to cost me to have this shrink tell you I'm to blame for everything?"

How about that? Finally, an honest area for discussion. After Ron left, I asked Becky if she felt like continuing the session. She tearfully nodded. "I've got to try something before it's too late."

In the counseling sessions that followed, I learned that Becky and Ron were high school sweethearts who had married shortly after graduation. Her father was a pastor, and her mother sang in the church choir. The family often held Bible studies in their home. She remembers her dad as a kind and quiet man who seldom raised his voice. Becky added that her mother was very submissive to her father and, even today, she has never heard them argue.

Ron's family background was profoundly and predictably different. Becky said that Ron was six when his father left his wife for another woman. After about a year he angrily returned home, but only after losing his job and having nowhere else to go.

Becky recalls hearing Ron talk about how his father would yell at his mother. He would scream at her for not being a better housekeeper, for always looking haggard and tired, and for being a lousy cook. "My old man ruled with an iron fist. You didn't dare disobey or you'd pay for it," he proudly told Becky.

In later sessions we focused on Becky's *boundaries*—in other words, what she wanted and needed from Ron and from their marriage. I asked her to consider the next two questions carefully: "Are your expectations for your marriage reasonable and attainable? And what are you willing to do, or not do, to attain them?"

Becky was anxious to discover the answers to these questions —and others. She learned that it was OK to have needs and wishes. She learned that she was responsible only for her own happiness. Through therapy, she discovered a personal sense of "self"—something that had never been modeled for her at home.

Encouraged by her new-found assertiveness and ability to set limits, Becky requested that Ron enter counseling to begin working on his major control issues or she would leave. Ron reluctantly agreed. It was plain to see how Ron's childhood environment had contributed greatly to his rigid and controlling nature. Eventually, Ron would come to grips with this controlling pattern and work on methods to break out of the mold his father helped to set.

How Do You Know If You Are a Rigid and Controlling Parent?

The following fifteen questions have been designed to answer that question. Try to respond to each question honestly. Sometimes it is easier to answer the questions the way you think your spouse would answer them (about you). In fact, if you're really brave, give a copy of the test to your spouse and see if she agrees with your answers.

RIGID AND CONTROLLING PARENT SELF-TEST

(Circle YES or NO)

1. Do I often say no to my kids even though I could have said yes? YES NO

2. Do I often hear and react rather than listen and respond? YES NO

3. Do I often find it hard to believe my kids' side of the story? YES NO

4. Do I often find it hard or impossible to change my mind even when I know I should? YES NO

5. Do I sometimes have to resort to threatening my kids with punishment or intimidation to get them to do as they are told? YES NO

6. Do I sometimes find my children going to my spouse or others instead of to me when they are having problems? YES NO

7. Do I find it very difficult, or impossible, to admit my mistakes or apologize to my kids? YES NO

8. Do I often feel that my spouse is far too easy on the kids? YES NO

9. Do my kids cry easily when I talk to them about a problem? (Younger children only, or think back to when your teenagers were younger.) YES NO

10. Do I often feel that my children like my spouse better than me? YES NO

11. Do I think my children lie to me because they don't think I'll believe the truth? YES NO

12. Do I often find myself forcing my kids to do what I want through threats or by saying such things as "Because I said so, that's why." YES NO

13. Do I think my spouse undermines my authority in the family? YES NO

14. Do I feel as though I don't get the respect from   YES   NO
    my children that I deserve?

15. Do my children seem somewhat sneaky or   YES   NO
    avoid telling me things that they may be afraid I
    won't approve of?

Scoring Your Test

Add up the number of times you answered "YES" to the above questions and refer to the chart below for the scoring.

Number of YES Answers	Interpretation
3 or fewer	No need for alarm. You are probably not a rigid and controlling parent.
4–7	You are on the borderline of being a rigid and controlling platoon parent. Warning signs should be posted: DANGER, TRAINED ATTACK PARENT IN HOUSE.
7–10	There is a better than even chance that you are a rigid and controlling parent. Consider getting fitted for some green camouflage fatigues. You may want to begin working on a more balanced approach to parenting before your family hires a "hit man." Read on, and consider using a highlighter.
10 or more	Check your insurance plan for accidental death benefits. Consider hiring a food taster (preferably someone you've never met) and begin warming-up to the term *family counseling*.

Remember, rigid and controlling parents are about as welcome as ants at a picnic. But don't panic, there's hope.

How Do I Stop Being a Rigid and Controlling Parent?

Let's say that you scored a ten-plus on the rigid and controlling scale. What now? Be forewarned that you are more likely to disappear under mysterious circumstances than a "normal" parent. Of course, your grieving family will take a Caribbean cruise the weekend following your untimely departure, just to help them grieve your loss, of course.

Seriously, you have the power to serve notice on Platoon Leader and evict him from your parenting style. He's vulnerable, for example, to honesty and sensitivity. Hit him where it hurts. There are no pills or quick fixes, but the following five steps can give you a running start in the right direction.

Step One: Acknowledge That You Have a Problem

Whether it's alcohol, chocolate sundaes, or being a controlling parent, we must first acknowledge (confess to ourselves) that a problem exists. This consciousness-raising process is an important first step in forcing the problem out of hiding and into the light, where it can be examined, dealt with, and confessed to others. Once we've taken complete custody of the problem, known as "owning," we can move on to the recovery process.

Step Two: Confessing and Making Amends

First John 1:9 promises, "If we confess our sins, he is faithful and just and will forgive us our sins and purify us from all unrighteousness." Confessing our sins and transgressions is fundamental. It enables us to arrive at a place of forgiveness, reconciliation, and recovery. No, you don't need to call your Aunt Betty in Omaha and confess to being an evil, controlling parent. (She's no Parent-of-the-Year candidate herself.) It does require, however, that you meet individually with the people who have been affected by your rigid and controlling parenting style—your family. Let them know that you have identified a personal problem that you are striving to overcome.

Ephesians 6:4 instructs not to "provoke your children to anger" (NASB). As an experienced rigid and controlling parent, it's a safe bet that you've "picked fights" and provoked anger from your kids on countless occasions. Confess this to them. Yes, it's a humbling experience, but stop whining. Nobody said growth was going to be easy.

Step Three: Ask for Forgiveness

Now that you've confessed your problem, ask for forgiveness. This is an emotional prerequisite for recovering from a rigid and controlling parenting style. The fact that you are open enough to ask for forgiveness proves that you are on the road to recovery. Only a short time ago you would have been thoroughly repulsed by the idea of asking for a child's forgiveness. Though divulging any weakness is a scary thought for a controlling parent, it's a mandatory hurdle that must be cleared on the way to becoming a more balanced parent.

Step Four: Make a Commitment to Change

After you've asked for forgiveness, don't delay in making a commitment to change. It's not like some household chore you've been putting off for months, such as cleaning the garage. It's easy to say on Tuesday, for example, "Honey, I'm going to clean the garage this weekend." As the weekend draws closer, however, your golf clubs are beckoning: "8:45 tee time; be there." The garage can wait.

Making a commitment to change is where the "rubber meets the road"—or as your spouse might say, "Put up or shut up." Once you've committed to change and have asked for forgiveness, be prepared to ask for their support as well. You're going to need all the help you can get to keep that positive momentum rolling.

Don't fall into the trap of saying, "If only you'd do what I want more often, I wouldn't be so controlling." Too bad there's no parenting referee in your house at this point, because he would be blowing his whistle and tossing his penalty flag into the air: "Fifteen yards for emotional withholding. Fourth down!" Anytime you hear the words "if only" beware, someone is trying to control you.

If you're serious about your commitment to change, a conversation with your children might begin with, "I understand that I have been very rigid and controlling with you." (You may have to substitute other words depending on the ages of your children. "Numbskull" and "bonehead" have a nice ring.) "I'm trying to make some changes, and I will probably need your help. If you think I'm being unfair, rigid, or controlling, you have my permission to let me know."

If you're already breaking into a cold sweat at the prospect of asking your kids for this kind of input, remember that asking them to "tip you off" doesn't mean that you're now compelled to change your mind. It means that you are willing to stop, look, and listen to their opinions with an open mind.

Again, don't try to make these changes alone. Get your family involved with the healing process. After all, aren't we all more likely to do something that requires discipline—such as attending aerobics class three times a week—if we know a friend is going to join us?

Step Five: Get Support While
You Are Making Personal Changes

We break commitments every day: that movie you promised to take your kids to see, and didn't; the friend who you told you would call more often, and haven't; the dentist appointment you missed, rescheduled, and missed again. So why shouldn't emotional commitment to change be just as difficult to keep? There are several proven methods for increasing the odds of keeping commitments. While Step Four (accountability) is certainly the first line of defense, other methods may also be helpful.

☐ *Books and tapes*
There are a myriad of excellent materials available to parents. Remember, no single book or tape has all the answers. Keep your eyes and ears open. Read it all. Watch it all. And you'll rapidly gain insight as to what materials may be beneficial for you and which can be left on the shelf.

☐ *Counseling support groups and friends*
Churches, PTAs, schools, and hospitals frequently offer parenting seminars. Contact your neighborhood church, or consult the yellow pages for the parenting support groups in your area. You may also have a friend who shares similar parenting issues. Get together with him or her on a weekly basis for mutual support, encouragement, and accountability.

☐ *Counseling*
There's no shame in seeking help with problematic parenting issues. Some specific problems can be addressed with as few as one or two visits. Pastoral counseling can also be very helpful in working through family issues.

THE OPPOSITE OF THE PLATOON PARENT:
THE OVERLY PERMISSIVE, OR PUSHOVER, PARENT

The second most effective way to alienate your kids is to be a pushover parent. They are often people who bought hook, line, and sinker into the fifties and sixties parenting approach. Parents were instructed to go easy on the reprimands, and, for heaven's sake, "Don't spank!" because it would cause permanent damage to their little psyches—as if their psyches are geographically housed in the region where you spank them.

Some pushover parents believe that the best way to parent their children is to be a "best friend," whereas others simply can't bring themselves to set limits or provide structure. They believe that spanking, scolding, or any consequence of discipline will harm a child's self-esteem. When you get right to the heart of these parents' motives, you often find that they are more concerned with avoiding their own feelings of guilt when setting limits. Setting limits and following through with consequences often makes them feel insecure about how much their children will like them—a major motivator. A typical crushing thought for the pushover parent is, *My kids may grow up not liking me if I'm too strict.*

Many people think that children, especially teenagers, would prefer to have a pushover parent. The truth is, however, that pushover parents confuse their children by not providing the guidance, accountability, and structure they so desperately need. The permissive parent feels that he must be the consummate diplomat. Negotiate and reason before discipline. If all else fails, keep negotiating.

For some reason, the local supermarket seems to attract pushover parents. A child is pitching a major fit at the check-out line because his parent said no (perhaps for the first time) to the child's demand for a candy bar. Spanking (perish the thought) is out of the question. For some parents, an intimidating stare would be enough to levitate the child right off the floor. Others would firmly, but gently, hold onto the child's hand until safely within the confines of the family minivan. The permissive parent, though, will attempt to reason and negotiate with the child by sharing their feelings about the candy bar situation. Finally, the child gets the candy bar and goes into a victory dance right there at the checkout counter. Like the Energizer Rabbit, the problem goes on, and on, and on.

Pushover parents often develop a parenting style based on their own limitless, boundaryless, and permissive childhoods. Since there are no "real" consequences for inappropriate behavior, compliance becomes an option in the child's mind. As a result, kids from this type of home have little regard or respect for the parent's needs and wishes or for the feelings of others. They become too wrapped up in their own self-centered neediness to notice.

Children who grew up in homes with one or two pushover parents often develop very distinct and troublesome personality traits. They tend to be self-centered, narcissistic (I am all-powerful, and the world revolves around me), and lacking in responsibility. In clinical terms, they are spoiled rotten. Since they never learned to respect authority in childhood, they often have difficulty with authority figures in adult life, such as teachers, coaches, police officers, or employers. Sadly, these children often wind up having difficulty enjoying and maintaining healthy relationships and marriages.

THE OVERLY PERMISSIVE PARENT SELF-TEST

Do you think you might have pushover tendencies? Answer the following ten questions and find out. Again, like the quiz for rigid and controlling parenting styles, try to answer them as objectively as possible.

1. Do you often blame your child's poor behavior on somebody else's bad influence, such as a spouse or neighbor kid? ☐ TRUE ☐ FALSE

2. Do your children often disregard your requests of them, such as to clean their rooms, get their homework done, or do other chores? ☐ TRUE ☐ FALSE

3. Do you sometimes use the line, "Wait till your father gets home"? ☐ TRUE ☐ FALSE

4. Do you hardly ever say no to your kids, and, when you do, do you feel guilty and try to make it up to them? ☐ TRUE ☐ FALSE

5. Are you quick to apologize or back down from any display of anger directed toward your kids? ☐ TRUE ☐ FALSE

6. Are you quick to give in to your child's wants, demands, temper tantrums, and wishes? ☐ TRUE ☐ FALSE

7. Do you often feel that your husband (or wife) is too strict, harsh, or short-tempered with the kids? ☐ TRUE ☐ FALSE

8. Do you find yourself buying toys or gifts for your kids even though it's not in the budget, nor is it a special occasion, but you feel they deserve it? ☐ TRUE ☐ FALSE

9. Do you find it difficult, or impossible, to stick to the rules you and your spouse set for your kids? ☐ TRUE ☐ FALSE

10. Do you often put your child's wants and wishes ahead of yours or your spouse's? ☐ TRUE ☐ FALSE

Scoring Your Test

Add up the number of times you answered "TRUE" to the questions and refer to the chart below to see how you did.

Number of TRUE Answers	Interpretation
2 or less	You are within the normal range of most caring parents. Even though you may have answered "TRUE" to less than three questions, you are probably able to identify when you are being a pushover parent and you are usually able to adjust in time.
3–5	You have one foot across the borderline for being a pushover parent and the other foot is on a banana peel. You have some backbone, but it likely turns to Jell-o when you are put to the test. Read on; you should begin working on a more balanced approach to parenting.

6 or more No offense, but your backbone is mostly made of marshmallow. You probably get nervous eating seafood because, as a jelly fish, you realize you are all in the same family. You may want to consider buying a big, ugly, mean dog to help you restore order to your home. Just teasing. There's hope! Read on.

Jim's Story

Jim, sixteen, was a handsome, intelligent teenager who was referred to me by the county probation department. Since his parents had divorced when he was three, Jim lived alone with his mom in a typical middle-class neighborhood. He visited his father only one week each year during summer vacation.

Jim was introduced to the criminal justice system when he was caught by the police trying to pass stolen checks at the mall. At the police station, Jim admitted to breaking into a neighbor's house with two of his friends and stealing several thousand dollars in property, plus the checkbook.

In our early sessions, Jim related that his mother never seemed to care about his activities or friends. "She didn't seem to mind whether I got B's or D's in school," he said. "She was always worried about making me angry, so I learned that I could get anything either by being real nice or by acting mad. When I got arrested, she wouldn't even believe that it was my fault, even though I told her it was all my idea. She believed that it must have been the bad influence of some of my friends."

It became obvious in our first few sessions that if you had looked up "pushover parent" in the dictionary, you would have found a picture of Jim's mom. She hadn't started out that way but had unwittingly fallen into the permissive trap due to several circumstances in her life. Let me explain.

After her divorce, she relied on her son for companionship. She also believed that her marriage had failed because of her own shortcomings. She should have been nicer, prettier, more appreciative, less critical, and more tolerant. As a result, she subconsciously began evolving into a permissive parent to avoid a similar failure with her son. Her deep-seated fear that Jim would one day abandon her, as his father had done, began to change the way she related to her son. She adopted a codependent philosophy of not making waves. If she were nice to Jim—making his life as perfect as possible—he would have no reason to leave, she subconsciously reasoned.

CAUTION! THESE CONDITIONS TEND TO CREATE PUSHOVER PARENTS

As we have seen, divorce can create such anxieties and insecurities that some people quickly lose sight of their original balanced parenting objectives. Other common influences leading to a pushover parenting style include

- Parents with codependent tendencies (similar to Jim's mom).
- Parents who came from permissive homes as children.
- Parents who came from controlling and rigid homes as children.
- Parents whose children may have been quite sick when young.
- Parents who had children unusually late in life.
- Parents with older children who have another child unexpectedly. (These children are sometimes smothered and overprotected not only by Mom and Dad but by older siblings as well.)
- Passive parents with strong-willed children.
- Children raised by grandparents.

Help for the Pushover Parent

For the pushover parent, as for the rigid and overly controlling parent, there's hope. You can change. The most effective method for enacting change is to follow the same "blueprint for recovery" that was effective for our platoon parent.

1. Acknowledge that you have a problem.
2. Confess and make amends.
3. Ask for forgiveness.

4. Make a commitment to change, and communicate that commitment to your kids.
5. Get support while you are making personal changes.

Changing personal parenting styles is never easy. Indeed, we are creatures of habit that naturally bridle against anything that remotely resembles change. With desire and motivation, even the most entrenched platoon or pushover parents can dramatically improve their parenting styles. You can change too!

THE WELL-BALANCED PARENT

If you are like most caring parents, you're probably concerned that you appear to have a few traits belonging to both problematic parenting styles. There's no cause for alarm. A well-balanced parent utilizes both parenting styles from time to time. The difference is, however, that this parent brings a balanced perspective to the task of parenting. He knows when to be a little on the controlling side, and when its OK to be permissive.

Let's look at the basic ingredients that go into the making of a balanced parent. A balanced parent is

- Loving
- Forgiving
- Consistent
- Communicative
- Fair
- Firm

Sounds a little like a Cub Scout oath, doesn't it?

Loving

Why do some parents have difficulty saying "I love you" to their children? Strange as it may seem, it's not uncommon for many parents to find it nearly impossible to verbalize their love. Generally, this type of parent was raised in a home where the parents were less than demonstrative in the love and affection department.

A good friend and co-worker of mine has two teenage boys. They are both rugged, athletic, and excellent students. On occasion,

I've been in his office when one of his boys happens to call. Without exception, he ends the conversation with "I love you too, son."

Unconditional love and acceptance is never an issue for balanced parents. A solid foundation of love, which includes grace, allows children to experience all the pain, disappointment, and heartache associated with growing up without being fearful of losing their parents' love.

Along with this foundation of love comes friendship. The balanced parent has the ability to be a friend to their child while always maintaining the boundaries, perspective, and positioning of a parent.

There are times during any parent/child relationship when feelings can become frayed. As long as there is an open line of communication between you and your kids, it's OK to be mad or to momentarily dislike each other.

Forgiving

If you live in a two-story house, you've probably witnessed the delightful sight of your child sitting at the top of the stairs, dejectedly poking his head though the rails. His expression is not unlike the one on your dog's face when you find that he's been rooting around in the trash most of the night. It can best be described as a "Do you still love me?" look.

With our kids, "the look" appears shortly after we have been pushed to our limits and have sent the little fire starters to their respective rooms (the "penalty box" in my home) to consider their transgressions (as if that's what they're going to do). After a few minutes without toys (or thirty minutes with multiple toys), they assume the stairway position awaiting just one thing from you—your forgiveness. After a tough day of breaking things, terrorizing the neighborhood, and thoroughly wreaking havoc, a child needs to know that he is still OK with you.

The balanced parent forgives unconditionally, but with eyes wide open. They realize that their kids are human, fallible, and fully capable of—even proficient at—making mistakes. A balanced parent knows how to address inappropriate behavior without being hurtful, critical, or minimizing. The child knows he is unconditionally accepted, despite the fact that he sometimes does bad things. His behavior may have been bad, but he's still a good kid. The balanced parent knows how to keep the negative behavior separate and apart from the child's overall feeling of self-esteem.

Sure, he tried to rinse the hamster off by dunking him in the toilet. The act was bad, but the intent was honorable. As a forgiving parent, your child knows that he can come to you even when he's really messed up. He knows that when it's all over you will offer forgiveness and guidance, not condemnation. If your kids can't approach you when they've messed up, how can you expect them to tell you when they're tempted by drugs, alcohol, or sex during their teenage years?

Consistent

Balanced parents are positively predictable through their consistent track record. Predictability is a bad thing for a criminal, but it is a tremendous strength in parenting.

In order to better understand the power of consistent and predictable parenting, let's examine what happens when consistency is missing from a parent's style. In this particular case, I met with a teenager whose parents sent him to counseling after he was caught cutting school several times. The first time he cut school, his parents angrily grounded him for a week but relented and allowed him go to a school dance. He cut school two weeks later while his dad was on a business trip. When his father returned, his mom had forgotten about the incident and there were never any consequences. Not surprisingly, he cut school a third time. This time his parents took away his allowance, sent him to therapy, and grounded him for two months. The issue here isn't so much the severity of the punishment, it's the "crazy making" inconsistency.

During a recent family outing to Sea World, I saw a fundamental example of parental consistency in action, only between man and dolphin. Hours before the main show was to begin in the giant pool, I noticed a trainer working with two young dolphins. He was preparing them for the day when they would mature into the first-string performers. A process, I later learned, that can take years. As I watched, a clear pattern developed. Each time one of the dolphins made an honest attempt to follow the trainer's command, he was rewarded with a fish. Not once did the trainer forget to dole out a prize for doing well or making an effort. Sea mammals, like kid mammals, learn best when provided with consistent and predictable reinforcement. A word of caution, however—most kids don't respond well to sardine incentives. It makes for some really awful breath, and it's nearly impossible to get the scales out of their hair.

In contrast, unpredictable and inconsistent parents (and dolphin trainers) confuse their children by making them continually guess what rules they are to follow. Children have a much greater chance of meeting your expectations when they know in advance what is expected of them.

Communicative

Let's give credit where credit is due. Moms are extraordinary communicators. When provoked, however, they have the amazing ability to punctuate each word with a cuff to the back of the head: "Now [smack] I [smack] told [smack] you [smack] . . ." Dads—don't try this at home. You'll probably pull a muscle.

Balanced parents are master communicators, a skill not lost on the business world. In the forties and fifties, many business studies were conducted to assemble a practical, working model for corporate communication skills. For a business to be successful, they learned, there had to be an "upward" flow of communication in addition to the traditional "downward" flow. In order for workers to feel valued and respected, there had to be a mechanism for their ideas, wants, and complaints to be conveyed. Some businesses scoffed at the idea, but others immediately began changing. Those that changed realized greater potential from their employees, which translated into higher productivity, greater job satisfaction, less turnover, and less employee sick time.

This upward communication concept is even more important in the family. The balanced parent welcomes and values input on decisions that affect the child and the family, just as a smart employer welcomes suggestions about issues that affect the company and its employees.

Balanced parents continually communicate their needs, wishes, wants, expectations, boundaries, and values to their children. This is best done in an open manner that encourages dialog between parent and child. As you might expect, this approach reduces much of the guesswork from being a child.

Relax—don't burst a vessel. Before you say, "This guy is crazy if he thinks I'm going to consult with my kids before making any decisions," let me explain. Opening the lines of communication doesn't mean that your kids get to wear the sergeant stripes in the family. The most powerful part of good communication skills is in its "valuing" effect. By making your kids part of the decision-making process, they will realize enhanced measures of self-esteem, empowerment, and responsibility—even if they don't get their way. Compliance is always easier for children when they feel invested in the decision-making process.

Fair

Did you ever marvel at the way a six-year-old can stretch a one-syllable word into five minutes? "THAT'S NOT FAAAIIIRRR!" I've gone to work with her uttering those infamous words, spent a hard ten-hour day, and walked back in the door as she's just completing the final exclamation point. And they stand there, with their little hands on their little hips, and repeat the phrase every time a ruling goes against them.

"No, honey, no ice cream for breakfast."

"THAT'S NOT FAAAIIIRRR!"

To the balanced parent, fairness goes hand in hand with firmness and consistency. Being a fair parent means hearing your child's side of the story before making arbitrary or hasty decisions. Being fair also means being able to change your mind when you hear new evidence that warrants consideration. In contrast, the controlling parent seldom, if ever, hears (or looks for) opposing points of view. Even if some mitigating evidence surfaces, he's dead set against changing his decision for fear he will appear weak.

Fairness, however, is never an issue for the pushover parent. Since that type says OK to almost everything, the child knows he can change the parent's mind with little effort.

Finally, a fair, well-balanced parent can apologize when he's wrong. Can you imagine how hard it is to get a platoon parent to (1) entertain the concept of being wrong, and (2) admit it? Conversely, the pushover parent often apologizes just to avoid conflict, even when he's probably right. It is easy to see the devaluing effect that both styles can have on a child's sense of what is fair.

Firm

The cereal aisle at the local supermarket may be the best place in the world to study child psychology. Sixty percent of all begging, moaning, and pleading occurs in the cereal aisle of supermarkets around the world. And don't think grocery stores haven't analyzed this very subject. Notice how they position certain products at kids' eye-level? It tells you who they are appealing to.

I would consider myself a fairly balanced parent—most of the time. Even so, I find it difficult to traverse the cereal aisle without at least one confrontation with my son over whether to buy his Teenage Mutant Ninja Turtle cereal or my Fruit Loops. "Fruit Loops again? THATS NOT FAAAIIIRRR!"

The easiest way to spot a parenting problem is by watching their reaction when the begging begins. Begging escalates depending on the situation. Children often begin with the simple yet effective "Pleeezzze." If that doesn't work, they take a stab at manipulation: "I'm not going to be your friend anymore," or, "I don't love you anymore." Others haul out the heavy artillery, which consists of crying, screaming, and the ever-popular holding of breath. My personal favorite is when they grab whatever they want from the shelves and hide it in your cart under the lettuce while your back is turned.

As well-honed as a child's manipulative skills may be, the balanced parent quickly, firmly, and appropriately confronts any unacceptable behavior. The Bible teaches us that ignoring problems will only lead to more problems. As it says in Matthew 18:15, "If your brother sins against you, go and show him his fault, just between the two of you. If he listens to you, you have won your brother over." The same holds true for parents. Ignoring your children's problems and manipulations will make confronting a similar behavior more difficult at a later date.

A Final Perspective
on the Three Parenting Styles

Whether you have identified yourself as a rigid and controlling parent, an overly permissive parent, or a balanced parent, there is only one central theme—to consistently and continually strive to be a more balanced parent.

Achieving and maintaining a balanced parenting style is at least an eighteen-year job. The real payoff comes when you see your child growing up to be a loving, responsible, well-balanced person with healthy self-esteem.

Above all, don't be too hard on yourself. Just do your best, and you'll do fine. Remember, whenever you feel yourself reaching the end of your rope, reach up, tie a knot, and read on—help is on the way.

What's my spouse's role in all this? When you hear the old adage "Opposites attract," it's generally used to describe people in a relationship, right? As true as this statement is for relationships, it is even more pronounced in parenting styles.

Whenever I speak to groups of parents, I confess to the audience that my wife and I once had opposite parenting styles. I used to be a little on the controlling side—OK, platoon parent to the tenth power. And she was a bit of a pushover—OK, cream puff. Our kids, of course, must have been well on their way to being schizophrenic. Seriously, we came from very different parenting camps, and it was confusing for our children.

The more research I conduct into parenting styles, the more inconsistencies I find between parents. It is very common, for instance, that a family contains both a controlling and a permissive parent. They were probably attracted to attributes they admired in the other but lacked in themselves. A strict, unemotional, and insensitive guy, for example, might be attracted to a forgiving, emotional, and sensitive girl. Sounds like one of those ads in the "personals" section: "SUI male seeking a FES girl. Must be a nonsmoker."

Diagnosing a problem is relatively simple. Implementing and motivating change requires hard work. Experience has taught me one thing: You can absolutely, positively, successfully change your parenting style with only one caveat—you must want to.

2

If You Really Want to Alienate Your Kids . . .
DON'T WORRY ABOUT THE WAYS YOU COMMUNICATE

A humorist once wrote that there's nothing so baffling as child training: "No sooner have you taught a child to talk than you have to teach him to be quiet."[1]

Once infants discover the power of communication, they embrace it like a warm blanket fresh from the dryer, and they never let it go. Remember when you were a newborn parent? How did you respond when your baby cried? You immediately answered the siren by meeting his most basic needs, right?

It wasn't long before your baby, already an honors student in Advanced Parent Training, discovered the "cause and effect" principles of communication. He cries, he gets fed. He cries, he gets held. He cries . . . "Say, this isn't too bad. All I have to do is cry and . . . hey, what about these diapers? Don't everybody volunteer at once."

Less fortunate children whose parents failed to meet these basic needs often experience tremendous fears, anxieties, and insecurities that chase them throughout their adult lives. Suffice it to say, communication between parent and infant is at the core of healthy child development.

As your baby matured, he intuitively learned the power of nonverbal communication. When he smiled or laughed, he couldn't help but notice that Mom and Dad were smiling and laughing, too. *Huh, is this a coincidence, or what?* he thinks. *Was it something I said?* Then things became clear. After soiling his diaper he watched in amazement as Mom swung into action with the speed of a fire brigade, while Dad fled from the room in horror. *No, this wasn't happenstance,* he decides. *This is pure talent.*

Your child had mastered the ability to satisfy his most fundamental needs through four basic communication modes—laughing, smiling (not to be confused with gas), moving, and making sounds (again, not to be confused with gas). Amazing, isn't it? Babies know exactly how to get what they need without uttering a single word.

There is no more powerful child-rearing tool than communication. In the right hands this tool can work wonders. In the wrong hands it can alienate with pinpoint accuracy. For parents, the key is to communicate what's in your heart—a message of love, limits, grace, tolerance, respect, and understanding. That's all your kids need to hear.

As well-balanced parents, the most important gift we can provide is an open environment that welcomes and includes our children as active participants in meaningful communication. Yet, nearly all of the parenting problems I encounter in the course of my practice—or under my own roof, for that matter—can be traced directly to power outages in the lines of communication.

Effective communication relates directly to positive parenting. As with any other business, there are tricks to the trade of parenthood—proven techniques to explore, opportunities to exploit, and land mines to avoid. All designed to restore or enrich the power of communication in your family—or, possibly, to switch it on for the first time.

To put it another way, if you're interested in alienating your kids, don't worry about the ways you communicate.

"Oh, No! I've Turned into My Mother!"

Certain physical traits are often passed down from one generation to the next. Unfortunately, so are poor communication skills. You can't do much about the unsightly toes you inherited from your mother, but there is a great deal you can do to improve the quality of communication between you and your children.

For nostalgia's sake, let's dust off some of those old standards on the parenting play list—popular one-liners that never go out of style, but should have become obsolete along with the Edsel. How old were you when you heard these quips?

"Because I told you so, that's why."
"Why don't you act your age?"
"Just wait until your father gets home."
"You'll never amount to anything."
"Is that the best you can do?"
"Where did we go wrong?"
"Why can't you be more like your sister?"
"Do I have to do *everything* for you?"
"If all your friends jumped off a cliff, would you jump too?"

If any of these golden oldies remain part of your parenting vernacular, read on.

Active vs. Passive Communication

It might be helpful to imagine yourself as the parent in the following two scenarios. How would you react or respond?

Susie, a thoughtful thirteen-year-old, arrives home from school to find her mom clipping coupons at the kitchen table. Apprehensive about interrupting her work, she says nothing but stands quietly by the table where her mom is virtually hidden by a growing mountain of double-savers. Finally, Susie's mom acknowledges her presence.

Act One:

MOM: "Hello, Susie. How was school today?" she says glancing up for a second.

Susie: "OK, I guess," she says softly as Mom goes back to cutting coupons. "A girl in my class got in trouble for having drugs in her purse when the teacher found them. The police came and took her away."

Mom: "Oh, that's terrible! But I suppose she got what she deserved for bringing drugs to school in the first place," she adds without missing a snip.

Susie: "I guess so," she says sadly, before going to her room to change.

Act Two:

Mom: "Hello, Susie. How was school today?" she asks, immediately setting down her scissors to give Susie her full attention.

Susie: "OK, I guess. A girl in my class got caught with drugs in her purse—the teacher found them. Then the police came and took her away."

Mom: "Oh, how sad," she responds with empathy. "How well do you know the girl?"

Susie: "She's in three of my classes. You know, Mom, I thought she was a nice girl."

Mom: "How did it make you feel to find out she was using drugs?"

Susie: "I think it scared me a little—she seemed so normal and nice."

Mom: "How common do you think it is for the kids at your school to have drugs, Susie?"

The mom in Act Two seized the opportunity to enter into a meaningful conversation with her daughter about drugs and the kids at school. As a result, the door was swung open to further discussions concerning the dangers of drugs, personal values, and choices.

By contrast, our Act One mom threw one monkey wrench after another into the gears of communication. While making only momentary eye contact with Susie, her comments lacked sensitivity, and her questions required mere one-word answers. She was obviously more interested in saving fifty cents on a box of Frosted Flakes than truly communicating with her own daughter. This is known as passive communication.

Effective communication utilizes leading statements—questions or requests to generate further conversation. For example, when Susie's mom asked in Act Two, "How well do you know the girl?" she succeeded in drawing her daughter into a deeper conversation centered on her personal experiences. She showed genuine interest and empathy by asking questions that provoked more thought and conversation. She also recognized an opportunity to dialog with Susie about her knowledge of drugs.

COMMUNICATIONS SYMPTOMS

When your child begins coughing and sneezing, it's a safe bet that he or she is coming down with a cold or allergy flare up. You quickly take the appropriate action to treat these symptoms. Similarly there are also clear indicators associated with good or bad communication, symptoms that could lead to a breakdown in that area.

In the box below, put a check mark next to the statements that fit your situation. You may want to refer back to these statements as you get a better understanding of how to treat communication ailments with your kids.

SYMPTOMS OF *GOOD* COMMUNICATION BETWEEN CHILD AND PARENT

☐ Child establishes eye contact when talking.
☐ Child doesn't become defensive when questioned.
☐ Child readily admits mistakes.
☐ Child asks for forgiveness when he is wrong.
☐ Child doesn't depend on lying and manipulating to get his way.
☐ Child is able to talk about and describe her feelings.
☐ Child communicates his needs and wishes.
☐ Child is respectful and listens without interrupting.
☐ Child asks questions when she doesn't understand the parent's viewpoint.
☐ Child seldom loses her temper during a disagreement.
☐ Child can agree to disagree on points that have been discussed to their logical limits.

Symptoms of *Poor* Communication Between Child and Parent

- ☐ Eye contact is seldom established between child and parent.
- ☐ Child is defensive and argumentative, especially when positions are challenged.
- ☐ Child is unwilling to admit mistakes, even in the face of irrefutable evidence.
- ☐ Child will not ask for forgiveness, even when he knows he's wrong.
- ☐ Child will lie to get out of a "sticky" situation.
- ☐ Child is unwilling to talk about her feelings because she feels nothing positive will come of it.
- ☐ Child fails to make his needs known because he doubts he will be heard.
- ☐ Child constantly interrupts because she doesn't respect others.
- ☐ Child will not attempt to clarify a question because extending the conversation isn't worth the effort.

Sex, Drugs, and Forbidden Fruit

As parents, it's our responsibility to speak with our kids about the tough subjects. This doesn't mean talking about the fine art of laying down a drag bunt or learning how to order a ceramic doll from the Home Shopping Network. I'm talking about drugs, alcohol, sex, and dating.

God didn't waste any time tackling the tough subjects. He began at the very outset—in Genesis 2:16–17. He tells His children, Adam and Eve, "You are free to eat from any tree in the garden; but you must not eat from the tree of the knowledge of good and evil, for when you eat it you will surely die."

How many of us parents would have said, "I'm not comfortable talking to my kids about this fruit thing. After all, it's only one tree, and it's way over on the next block. They may not even find the tree. And if they do, the fruit is probably well out of reach. I'll discuss the fruit problem when they get a little older. Anyway, I heard that that snake can talk; he'll probably tell them about it."

God could have been like many of us and said nothing. He could have waited. He knew, however, that it was His responsibility to communicate the risks involved with forbidden fruit.

Some parents find it easier to delay or avoid talking about the tough subjects. In doing so, however, they're leaving it up to the "snakes" in this world to do the talking for them. And when it comes to drugs, alcohol, AIDS, sex, and dating—none of us want that.

When should parents begin talking to their kids about difficult issues? In general, when your child begins to express an interest or communicates curiosity about a particular subject.

If you've been putting off a few choice subjects until the time is right or until you feel more comfortable with the topic, I urge you to delay no longer. There are usually two reasons that parents avoid the tough subjects: they are either scared or uninformed, or both.

A good way to approach any difficult or "touchy" topic is to first ask your child what he knows about the subject. It may surprise you that even five- and six-year-olds are savvy about drugs, for instance. Next, consider taking your kids on a fact-finding mission to the public library. Check out a couple of books and do some reading together. Not only does this show *your* willingness to learn and teach it right, it affords an opportunity for quality time.

THE WHAT AND WHENS OF TOUGH SUBJECTS

Often, during parenting lectures, I am asked to outline the specific ages parents should open a dialog with their kids on difficult subjects. The following chart is to serve as a guideline only. Remember, you are the only expert on your child. It's up to you to decide the best time to discuss any particular subject.

Subject	Approximate age
Strangers	3
Others touching you	4
Alcohol	5
Drugs	5
Smoking	5
AIDS (general)	7
Dating (setting dating rules)	7
Homosexuality (biblical & social perspective)	9
Premarital Sex (biblical & social perspective)	10
AIDS (specifics, i.e., transmission, risk group, etc.)	11

COMMUNICATING WITHOUT WORDS

So far we've talked about some verbal tools you can use to develop better communication skills with your kids. But remember that nonverbal communication tools can be equally as effective.

Being a Good Audience

Earlier we discussed the value of eye contact when speaking with your children. There are times, however, when the most powerful eye contact between parent and child has nothing to do with conversation.

Let's say your little leaguer is stuck out in right field. He already feels miles away from the action when a ball finally comes his way. Miraculously, he makes a leaping one-handed catch. He immediately looks in the direction of the stands where he hopes to see his parents applauding wildly. Instead, they are busy talking to other parents. They never saw his catch. They had dropped the ball when it came to nonverbal praising.

Unintentionally, these parents were communicating a minimizing message that said, "The game is boring, and we would rather be doing something else." That may be true, but you certainly don't want to communicate that to your children.

One day my daughter burst into the room trumpeting the exciting news: she had just learned a new routine in dance class. "Watch me, Mom!" she implored, as she began a spin that was making me dizzy.

Meanwhile, I noticed that my wife was engrossed in a TV miniseries. I almost said to Tracy, "Don't feel too bad. I couldn't get her attention if I ran through the house with my hair on fire." Just then, she turned down her program and watched my daughter pirouette through the living room. When her minirecital was finished, my wife applauded and hugged her. Tracy beamed. *Nice job, honey,* I thought. (Although I did catch her glancing at the TV each time my daughter's back was turned.)

There's a flip side to this story. What if your child fails to make eye contact with you? If this occurs repeatedly, you may want to probe deeper. I term lack of eye contact in children or teenagers a "shame-based response." In many cases, the child may be feeling ashamed, insecure, afraid, or perhaps he is not being totally truthful.

A Hug, a Kiss, and a Pat on the Head
(Pat your dog, but don't forget the kid)

When I was a kid, I was told to always give the family dog a pat on the head as I walked by. "It shows the dog you like him," my parents would say. After fifteen years of head patting we had the most well-adjusted dog on the block, but everyone else in my family needed some serious "couch time." Do you find yourself hugging and patting your pets more than you do your kids? Remember, what's good for a canine is good for the kid—except when it comes to flea collars, kibble, and wet noses.

Touching, and especially hugging, is a tremendously important form of nonverbal communication. Children should never get too old to hug. They may protest publicly as they mature, but, privately, hugging is still important to them. It will always be important, regardless of age.

A special note to fathers: Dads have a natural tendency to begin pulling away from hugging and "rough-housing" with daughters as they mature sexually. Since preteen and teenaged girls are already feeling insecure about their emerging sexuality, they need reassurance that your affection for them hasn't changed. Keep those hugs going.

COMMUNICATION IN ITS UGLIEST FORMS

As well-balanced parents we exercise tact, self-control, and authority in equal portions. Right, and the Easter Bunny will bring you two eggs this year.

Have you ever had this recurring nightmare? Your children grow up to be the kinds of people you didn't want your kids playing with. It's a frightening thought, one that usually surfaces after we've discovered that our kids have mastered yet another ugly form of communication.

Communication at its ugliest includes

- Lying
- Sulking
- Arguing
- Swearing
- Temper tantrums

Nothing new. Children and adults have been busy lying, sulking, arguing, swearing, and throwing temper tantrums since dinosaurs ruined picnics in the park. (And you thought ants were a nuisance!) I'm afraid the best we can hope for is awareness, while maintaining an active line of communication with our kids. Don't forget that kids often mirror the behavior they see at home. And there are times when "imitation isn't the sincerest form of flattery."

You might think, for example, that it's only a "little white lie" when you tell your wife, "If that's my boss calling, I'm not home." Unfortunately, your child doesn't make the same distinction. He sees it as lying—plain and simple. You've communicated a mixed message. "Why, he ponders, is it OK for Dad to lie, when I get my seat dusted for doing the same thing?"

Your children and teenagers also need to understand that in the heat of the moment people, not just kids, can lose self-control. We should emphasize the importance of getting a handle on the root causes of any outburst or "acting up." Whether it's lying, swearing, or threatening to drop the cat from the roof if all demands aren't met, it's only through understanding and open dialog that these verbal brush fires can be extinguished.

So cover your ears, and hold your nose—it's time to take a close look at communication at its ugliest. The following charts are intended to provide some insight into the cause and effect of various undesirable forms of communication. While examining these areas, remember that no two children are alike. These charts are designed to serve as a point of reference only. If questions arise, I suggest you consult a therapist who specializes in working with children or adolescents.

Truth, Lies, and Lincoln Logs

You've just witnessed your four-year-old deliberately drop a Lincoln Log into the toilet and applaud as it spins out of sight. When confronted, he emphatically swears it wasn't he. (Perhaps this is a combination of lying and self-preservation.)

A better example might be the time you found the keys to the Buick in your teenager's pocket. You calmly ask him about the new bay window that suddenly appeared in the garage door. He insists it wasn't he. (The long trail of garage door fragments leading directly to his room is a good tip-off that he's lying.)

Or picture this. Your child is crying, stomping his feet. He moans, "Noooo, I didn't have a donut before dinner." If he sticks to the story, you may have a problem, especially in light of the massive ring of powdered sugar around his mouth. Take a closer look at the motivating factors behind the lying before he gets too slick to catch in the act.

UGLY FORM NO. 1

Symptom	Lying
Root Cause	may have low self-esteem
	may be afraid of criticism
	may be feeling insecure
	may have overly controlling parents
	may have trouble with self-control
	may think with a victim mentality
	may feel that the truth is not heard
	may be feeling misunderstood
	may be feeling powerless

Most children between the ages of four and six go though stages of lying. It's often, but not always, a part of growing up. When your child lies about something, take the time to gather all the facts. Attempt to look past the lie and examine the fabric of his feelings. Did he feel, for example, that he was compelled to lie? Above all, take any lie seriously, although you may have to restrain your laughter when your kid fibs with powdered sugar all over his mouth.

Dr. C's Parenting Law Number 300235: There must always be consequences for lying, no matter how small or large. We'll talk more about the punishment fitting the crime in a later chapter, but lying must be addressed quickly. As you hand down the verdict, however, make sure your child knows that he's still OK. You still love *him*; it's the lying that's bad.

Take time to let your kids know that lying is a very serious subject in your family. A positive way is to hold a family Bible study on the behavior. There are many interesting verses in the Bible that address the consequences of lying.

Some Thoughts about Swearing

#%&¢$#&$@#&¢@%!!! Yipes! Out of the mouths of babes! Remember when your six-year-old uttered those immortal words at Aunt Ethel's birthday party? My first thought was that there must be a ventriloquist throwing his voice from the front yard. No, it was he all right. "Gather up Dillinger's stuff, dear. I think it's time to go home."

UGLY FORM NO. 2

Symptom   Swearing

Root Cause may be seeking attention
may be seeking peer approval
may be feeling rebellious
may have a lack of self-control
may have low self-esteem
may be unable to cope with anger
may not respect authority
may be trying to manipulate or intimidate
may be trying to gain control

You can usually trace the use of profanity in children between the ages of four and six to a sibling, a neighborhood kid, or something they picked up at school. Sometimes the trail is fresh and leads straight to Dad, who occasionally utters a profound gem as his team fumbles the ball for the second straight time. This discovery—by Mom—is usually followed by Speech No. 7, which concludes with, "Boy, are you a wonderful influence on your son. Why don't you just take him to the bowling alley for a few beers!"

Older children and teenagers will use profanity to punctuate a message. "That was a $%&#@C#$ football game Friday, wasn't it?" This essentially comes from a need for peer approval and acceptance. When profanity is employed as a rebellious tool or to show disrespect, however, it becomes more symptomatic of a troubled youth lashing out at others in anger.

FIVE STEPS FOR FIGHTING FOUL PHRASES

1 *Identify the root cause of the profanity and address it in an appropriate manner.* It's particularly important to look for insecurities and a need for peer acceptance. Begin by pointing out your child's good qualities. Help her understand that the use of profanity isn't consistent with her personality, the family standards, or her high standards as an individual.

2 *Ask him if he knows why he's been swearing.* Let him think this through. The better he understands his attraction to profanity, the easier it will be to break the habit.

3 *Communicate your family values to your children.* Let them see that profanity is not only a poor reflection on the family; it is worse than that. Be clear and firm that you want the swearing to stop.

4 *Set up a behavioral system.* Every time your kid utters a four-letter word, consider these two major motivators for kids: (1) slap her with a fine; (2) give her extra chores around the house. (For positive reinforcement systems, see chapter 8.)

5 *Let him also know that God has given us special commands about profanity, as well as about taking His name in vain.*

The Power of Protest

"Because I told you so . . . that's why." This is the ultimate and sometimes unavoidable escape clause for parents. Let's face it, you can argue with an eight-year-old until you're blue in the face. Could it be that children argue with their parents because they realize that time is on their side? They know who is going to be around longer. No, couldn't be.

UGLY FORM NO. 3

Symptom	Arguing
Root Cause	may be feeling excess anxiety
	may be disrespectful of authority

> *Root Cause*   may have low self-esteem/self-image
> may be feeling powerless
> may be seeking attention or control
> may be unable to cope with his anger
> may be exerting excess control
> may be using it as a defense to closeness
> may be afraid of criticism

When your eleven-year-old argues that he studied as hard as he could for the latest spelling test, while misspelling everything including his name, you know you've got a problem. There's no reason for debate; he should have studied harder. Period.

I can't overstate the importance of determining root causes, especially when it comes to a child's argumentativeness. Ask yourself these questions while he is protesting the loudest:

- ☐ Is he arguing with me out of his anger and defiance for my authority, which translates into resentment?
- ☐ Is he arguing with me because arguing and fighting seem to be a way of life in our house?
- ☐ Is he arguing with me because I am asking something of him that is unreasonable?
- ☐ Is he basically just an opinionated and stubborn kid?
- ☐ All of the above.

The origin of these outbursts often resides in feelings of resentment coupled with a sense of powerlessness.

When children argue for argument's sake they probably fall into several distinct categories. The first is the child who will argue with most anything you say.

PARENT: "You did your math homework wrong."
CHILD: "No, the teacher said I could do it that way."

This child stubbornly "digs in" and holds his position like a soldier in a fox hole. "The sun sets in the east," and that's that.

If stubbornness is common in your home be sure that you're not the prime target. Is he stubborn with everyone or just you? Perhaps you're so busy, the only way your kid can win your attention is through inappropriate behavior. He may believe that the only way to win your respect is by winning disagreements. Finally, he could be entering into conflicts as a method to assert his need for autonomy. He may be indirectly asking for more independence from your authority.

Other children argue as a defense to keep people from getting too close. They are often insecure kids with feelings of inadequacy. Symptoms can include tears, harsh words, hurt, anger, and a need to retreat into isolation. If your child exhibits symptoms such as these, look for ways to build her self-esteem.

When you can't find a clear reason behind your child's stubborn, arbitrary, argumentative, and disrespectful ways, you may want to look in the mirror before asking your wife, "How in the world did he get this way?" Remember, fruit doesn't fall far from the tree. He may be arguing because he's accustomed to the sounds of discord in the home.

Finally, some kids are simply predisposed to arguing. They're perfectionists. They're opinionated. They're strong willed. They're annoying. These are children who respond to everything with a negative:

The world is round. "Not perfectly."

That's a pretty blue dress you are wearing. "No, it's a greenish blue."

You're not my child, you were left here by aliens. "Was not!"

On Rare Occasions, Even Moms and Dads "Lose It"

I have a reputation for being cool under fire—an ice man when it comes to making tough decisions. But given the right set of circumstances, I have been known to "lose it" with the best of them. Only if provoked, mind you.

Not long ago my wife received an engraved invitation addressed "Occupant" to attend the grand opening of a new department store in our neighborhood. I'm certain they selected a construction site within easy range of her credit cards. I kept waiting for a department store limo to swing by and whisk my wife away.

UGLY FORM NO. 4

Symptom   Whining, moaning, and temper tantrums

Root Cause   may be trying to get more control
                  may be trying to manipulate
                  may be feeling angry
                  may be feeling anxious
                  may be feeling depressed
                  may be feeling misunderstood/unheard
                  may be feeling powerless
                  may be feeling lost
                  may have underdeveloped communication skills
                  may be that parents created the situation by
                       giving in to these outbursts in the beginning

---

Naturally, my wife had planned to be there a good hour before the doors opened. She also planned to take the eight-year-old fashion princess (a.k.a. Tracy) along. Her first words weren't "Daddy" or "Mommy." No, they were "paper or plastic?"

I called to my wife as she backed out of our driveway (eyes rolling back in her head as only a woman on the way to a sale can look). "Remember, the fashion princess has no money until allowance day. She's broke, you're broke, the country's broke, we're all broke!"

When they finally returned (I canceled the missing persons report), I watched in horror as they happily carried one bag after another from the van. "Need a wheelbarrow," I said under my breath.

I somehow managed to contain myself until after dinner, which meant I powered down my food in record time. Casually (like a leopard about to pounce) I asked my wife how Tracy had earned enough money to buy an entire wardrobe. "Wait, don't tell me," I said with sarcasm oozing like sap (and you know who the sap was). "You got her a job at the department store and these are samples, right?"

She quickly ambushed me with a look that meant one of two things: (1) You forgot our anniversary again; or (2) You're pushing your luck, fella; better back off if you ever expect to get a hot meal again. This would normally be warning enough, but not this time. Wasn't right on my side? Wrong.

"You're teaching our daughter that it's OK to buy things when she can't afford it—on credit," I fumed. "She shouldn't be allowed to take advances on her allowance. What in the world were you thinking about, honey?" The "honey" part was a nice touch but a little late. After a few weeks you get used to eating stuff out of cardboard boxes. What's wrong with Rice Krispies for dinner, anyway?

When your kid loses her temper, take the initiative to ask what's bothering her. Search out the underlying feelings and discuss them. Wait until emotions have settled, however, before tackling any highly charged root causes.

COMMUNICATION LAND MINES
(Trust me, large feet are a disadvantage in a mine field)

Men step on communication land mines (albeit accidently) more often than women. Why? Because they often keep their sensitivities stuffed away in an old shoe box somewhere between back issues of *Popular Mechanics* and their sixties baseball card collection.

Communication land mines are detonated regularly between you and your children, between you and your mate, between you and your boss, even between you and your dog. Or is that a different category of land mine?

Have you ever gotten up to get a cup of coffee, only to find your favorite donut missing? You immediately scream at the dog, who sits there—frozen—like a deer caught in your headlights. As you're reading the mutt his constitutional rights, you hear the sound of muffled snickers from down the hall—an unmistakable noise created when a six-year-old tries to laugh with an entire jelly donut stuffed in his mouth. *Kaaa boom!* Communication land mine.

"Sorry, Spottie. Here have a few donut holes. A little something to ease my guilt. And have a nice day."

Communication Land Mine No. 1:
Reacting vs. Responding

When we stumble over communication land mines it's typically because we've allowed our emotions to govern our actions. To put it bluntly, our mouth is in overdrive while our brain is in park. We're reacting instead of responding. Let's examine the differences between the two.

Reacting is an emotional form of communicating, whereas responding allows the thought process to become fully involved. It's important that parents be alert to the following warning signs before reacting emotionally:

☐ Does your face feel flushed?
☐ Have your listening skills shut down?
☐ Are you interrupting?
☐ Have you stopped listening and started formulating your reaction?
☐ Are you getting angrier by the second?
☐ Are you already thinking of punishment or consequences?

There's no simple solution to avoiding a reaction land mine. If you feel yourself about ready to explode, however, I suggest the following steps:

1. Stop.
2. Listen and ask clarifying questions.
3. Take a few deep breaths.
4. Call a time-out if you need one in order to gain your composure.
5. Get a second opinion if necessary.
6. Deal with the situation using love and logic instead of emotions and anger.
7. Remember, he's not a bad kid; it's just the situation that you're angry about.

Communication Land Mine No. 2:
Discounting Feelings

"When I want your opinion, I'll ask for it." Do you remember hearing your parents say that? Remember how minimizing and hurtful these comments felt? Discounting or minimizing a child's feelings is one of the most destructive communication land mines you can touch off. Discounting feelings is usually followed closely by an exploding sound and a ringing sensation in your ears—another land mine.

Remember that teenagers, kids, and even small children have a right to their thoughts, feelings, and opinions. They may be silly, pointless, and irrational, but they are valid nonetheless. Before you minimize, consider these questions:

1. Ask yourself if she seems to be more emotionally invested in this matter than you would normally expect her to be.
2. Ask clarifying questions such as, "Help me understand how you are feeling," or, "I don't think I'm seeing your side of this; can you help me out?" These questions will help you to get a clearer picture of the emotionally charged issues beneath the surface.
3. Be careful not to discount feelings by saying, "Don't feel that way," or, "I can't believe you are acting like this; it's not that big of a deal."
4. Validate his feelings by making statements such as, "You certainly have a right to feel the way you do," or, "I don't really understand what you are feeling, but I respect your right to feel that way."

Take the time to let your kids know that you respect and honor their feelings. God gives us the ability to have feelings, but nowhere does He give parents the authority to take them away. Even if we don't agree with or understand our child's feelings, remember that feelings are never right or wrong—they just are. Our child's feelings are part of his personal possessions and are not there for us to discount or discard.

Communication
Land Mine No. 3: Nagging

Men often nag their wives for what they do. Woman often nag their husbands for what they don't do. And parents? We just nag, nag, nag. At least that's the perception our kids have. What exactly is nagging? The *American Heritage Dictionary* defines it "To annoy by constant scolding, complaining, or urging." Fine, but how do you stop?

Do the following conversations sound familiar?

MOM:	"How many times do I have to remind you to pick up your room?"
CHILD THINKS:	"Well, that was number 1,346 this week, and I was sort of hoping it would be the last time."
MOM:	"I'd stop nagging you if only you would put your clothes away."
CHILD THINKS:	"I'd probably do better at putting my clothes away if you would quit nagging me so much."

Nagging is a lowly form of communication that seldom gets the job done. I've found that most parents (me included) nag because we feel our kids don't always take us seriously. That's true, especially if we're constantly nagging—vicious circle. It's a chicken-or-the-egg thing.

Our kids know through experience that they can get away with anything—at least twice—more often than that if they catch us with our defenses down, distracted on the phone, or if we're in a good mood because we're having a good hair day.

Poll a million kids on the subject, and roughly one million and two would say that their parents are world-class naggers. Wouldn't we be surprised if our kids compared nagging notes with their chums in fourth grade? I can see them gathered round the lunch tables swapping can-you-top-this stories. It might go something like this:

"Guess what? I got my mom to yell at me eight times for kicking the ball in the house," says one kid proudly.

"Break any windows?" asks another buddy. "No? Bummer, dude."

"That's nothing," shoots back another. "I got my mom to tell me eleven times to pick up my clothes—and then she picked them up for me. Don't I get bonus points for that?" High fives are shared all around.

Which one of the two following models for communicating house rules do you fall under?

THE NAGGING PARENT

Child	*You*
breaks a rule	tell him he broke a rule
breaks the rule again	tell him he did it again
breaks it a third time	tell him he did it again and ask him what's wrong with his head
stares at you wondering if you are really waiting for an answer	get tired of staring and go away shaking your head in frustration
goes back to terrorizing	go back into denial because you've lost control.

THE NONNAGGING PARENT

Child	*You*
breaks a rule	let him know the rule was broken and ask for his future cooperation
breaks the rule again	tell him you won't be nagging him about it any longer and you discuss the consequences if the rule is broken again
wonders if you've been replaced by a space alien	show him your driver's license and convince him it's still you
breaks the rule again	remind him of the rule and enforce the agreed upon consequences
	are in control

Bottom line: You don't have to be a nag if you are

- ✔ Consistent
- ✔ Firm but fair
- ✔ Able to follow through (and I don't mean your backhand). If you say it, mean it. If you don't intend to do it, don't say it.

We'll discuss how these rules apply to setting boundaries in chapter 5.

Communication Land Mine No. 4:
Forgetting to Catch Your Kids Doing Something Right

I first caught on to the trick of catching kids in the act of doing something right a few years ago while conducting a family therapy session. The parents complained that their two teenagers displayed a complete lack of regard for their authority by continually acting in a disrespectful manner.

It didn't take long to realize that the parents—although not exactly Mr. and Mrs. Platoon Leader—were often critical and insensitive to their children's emotional needs and feelings. Both Mom and Dad were raised by strict, critical, and somewhat emotionally detached parents. They grew up hearing, "Sure you got a B-average on your report card, but you should be getting A's. You should be studying harder."

When I met with the two teenagers alone in follow-up sessions, they disclosed that their parents never completely approved of anything they did. If it was chores, they could have done better. If it was homework, it could have been neater. In short, their parents were what I call "hypercritical parents"—basically fine people who had never learned that children need to hear positive stuff, too.

Be patient. You may have to wait a while before you catch your kids doing something right. There have been times when I've waited all day for them to do something praiseworthy. I've spent days stalking them around the house, like a half-crazed psychologist, just waiting to praise them. "Hurry up and do something praiseworthy. There it is . . . no, that wasn't it."

I recall one particularly barren day (just after Halloween) in the praiseworthy department. My daughter, like most eight-year-olds, would rather eat brussels sprouts than invite her little brother to go anywhere with her and her friends. We've had the usual assortment of father-daughter chats about how she needs to refrain from "ditching him" after calling the little guy "a complete geek" (like there are incomplete geeks).

As my daughter was preparing to go to her friend's house to categorize and alphabetize all their Halloween candy, I noticed my son sitting by himself, the picture of dejection. He looked like a kid who suddenly discovered that his trick-or-treat bag was full of apples, boxes of raisins, and a few sticks of peppermint gum. "Want to come with me to Courtney's, Matt?" she asked, catching him completely off guard. "You can have some of my candy." You could almost hear a band playing the "Hallelujah Chorus" as fireworks exploded overhead.

"Hey, Tracy," I called, recognizing this as a Kodak moment. "Come here for a minute." Have you ever noticed that every time you call your kids over—even when they've done something good— they look like a dog that's just dragged in something hairy and life- less? "Thanks for asking your brother to go with you. You're a pretty neat kid, and I'm proud of you."

As a rule of thumb, try to catch your kids doing something right at least twice as often as when you find them doing something wrong. Good hunting!

Communication Land Mine No. 5: Failing to Communicate Self-Esteem

As parents, we can help build our kids' self-esteem by reinforc- ing positive messages. I call these "esteem builders," and they should be given to your children like vitamins on a daily basis.

TWO TIES ARE BETTER THAN ONE

An associate of mine is continually arriving at work with not one, but two, ties. For weeks I said nothing. Finally, I broke down and asked him about it. He explained that one day he had asked his nine-year-old daughter to pick out his tie for the day. "She was so pleased that she now insists on making my tie selection every morning," he said. So now he wears "her" tie out of the house and takes another tie—one that isn't in the shape of a fish or has Mickey and Goofy on it—to wear once he gets to the office.

Asking questions, no matter how trivial they may seem to you, is a good way to bolster a kid's self-esteem—from the color of the new car you're considering to the ideal restaurant for lunch with your boss. Asking your kids for their input and opinions creates a feeling of self-worth and significance. It tells them that you respect and val- ue their opinions and that you are not above asking them for ad- vice—even if it means bringing two ties to work.

Communication Land Mine No. 6:
The I'm-Too-Busy Signals (Go away kid, you bother me)

"Not now. Can't you see I'm busy?" How many times have we used this communication crusher on our kids? Truth is, we have relatively few years to spend with our kids. They want and need us now, while they are small. When they become teenagers, we'll have to offer cash bribes just so they'll hang around with us for fifteen minutes.

Some common I'm-too-busy signals occur when

- ✓ You're reading the newspaper
- ✓ You're talking on the telephone
- ✓ You're enjoying your favorite television program(s)
- ✓ You're preparing dinner

Don't get me wrong. You'll eventually go crazy if you drop what you're doing each time your kids beckon—to say nothing about never finishing anything. I suggest, instead, setting and communicating realistic boundaries with your kids. (We'll take an in-depth look at boundaries and limits in chapter 5.)

My kids seem to sense when I'm on a deadline and will do their best to drag me away from the computer. I've got a choice to make. Either please my kids or disappoint my editor when I miss the deadline. Or I can begin communicating some boundaries. Looking straight into their needy little eyes I tell them, "I promised myself that I would write for the next hour. When that time is up, watch out, because I'm coming after you two, and you'd better be ready to play."

I have not only acknowledged their needs but communicated my own personal boundaries as well. They leave satisfied, knowing full-well you're going to be all theirs soon. Remember, nobody ever says on their deathbed, "I wish I had spent more time at work."

Communication Land Mine No. 7:
Pitting One Parent against the Other

Don't let them cut you from the herd. Stick together. There's strength in numbers. Kids have us pegged from head to toe. They're aware of our strong points, and they've also categorized and logged every chink in the armor. I can't prove it, but I think my daughter keeps a list of the sales pitches that have successfully evoked a yes from me after my wife has said no. Also beware of kids shedding tears, especially if she's just heard no from the mother half of this partnership.

Here's a situation that happened in my house just last week. My daughter came to me, bottom lip protruding, ticked off because her mother had said no to a slumber party. Knowing that nothing was planned on that particular night, I assumed that my wife must have another reason for turning down her request. Here were my options:

☐ I could overrule my wife's decision (not a wise move unless I enjoy food that only comes in Styrofoam containers).

☐ I can take the ball and run with it by asking my wife why my daughter can't go to the sleep over. The problem with this approach is that I would be assuming the role of the rescuer and my daughter would then expect me to do all her future dirty work.

☐ I could ask her how she approached my wife, and, if there was a breakdown in communication, I could suggest ways of reapproaching the subject.

My daughter and I discussed that her approach with her mom—tears, anger, and manipulation—was probably a poor tactical move. I encouraged her to try it again—only this time by using logic and reasoning.

My wife, of course, was aware (that's important) of this tactic. Tracy calmly asked her mom again about the overnighter, explaining why she felt so strongly about going. She also learned that unlike an umpire, parents are capable of changing their decision.

Even if your kids fail to overturn your judgment, it is important to give them some kind of a small victory if only to validate their change in attitude and behavior. Sometimes a reply such as this will work wonders: "I still don't want you to go to the sleep over because _____, but I sure appreciate the way you asked me about it this time."

Other object lessons were learned in this situation:

✔ Losing your temper doesn't accomplish anything.

✔ Seeking council to better understand a problem is wise.

✔ Appealing a decision is not such a scary thing, and you might even win.

✔ I can't pit one parent against the other, no matter how hard I try.

TAKING COMMUNICATION ON THE ROAD

Last, but certainly not least, we should address the issue of extended-range communication. Though my speaking engagements often require travel, it doesn't mean that the active line of communication I enjoy with my kids has to suffer. When I call home, I make it a point to ask about their day.

As you well know, most kids prefer to answer a parent's questions with a grunt, a shrug, and then a one-syllable word ("Fine," "OK"). Instead, try posing your questions this way: "What did you do in school today?" or, "Was the spelling test hard? I bet you don't remember the toughest word on the test," or, "What are you guys going to do later tonight?"

Again, don't be satisfied with one-word answers from your kids. Ask questions that require a complete-sentence response. You will not only find out what your child is up to (although you may not want to know), but you also convey real interest and a sense of esteem and importance.

Another trick is to leave little notes around the house before you leave town. Stick one under their pillows. Stash another in a lunch box or underneath the tooth paste (they'll never find it there). They can be funny notes or just a reminder of your love. Most important, you have made another connection. You're communicating. As your note-hiding techniques become more advanced, you can spread the note-finding surprises out for days. (By the way, don't be surprised if your kids start leaving little notes for you, too.)

3

If You Really Want to Alienate Your Kids . . .
MAKE THEM EARN
YOUR LOVE AND RESPECT

Let's face it, the closest most of us will ever get to perfection is when we're typing a résumé or filling out a job application. Can you imagine being completely honest? How would it look to admit, for instance, that you're always late for work? Or how about informing your prospective employer that you typically call in sick eight or ten times a year. "Not to worry, though, I'm really out shopping or fishing—or something."

And how about job interviews? We go to great lengths to beef up our strong points and carefully downplay any deficits. We have, after all, only a few minutes to convince a total stranger (who keeps looking at his watch) that we're the greatest thing since microwave popcorn.

Given our own inconsistencies and shortcomings, why do some of us demand perfection from, of all people, kids?

THE "WHAT HAVE YOU DONE FOR ME LATELY?" PARENT

Some parents run their families like the CEO of a Fortune 500 company. Productivity, punctuality, and performance—heaven help the kid who contributes to a poor quarterly household earnings report because he needed a tonsillectomy.

The "What have you done for me lately?" parent continually finds fault. He also finds it nearly impossible to compliment his kids. When he does, it usually comes in the form of "That's fine, but . . ."

> "That's fine, Billy. Our front lawn finally looks like the 18th hole putting green at Pebble Beach. But what about the palm trees in the backyard? You were supposed to shinny up and trim them last week."

> "Way to go, Jennifer—you scored two goals today. But you could have had three if you weren't daydreaming when that ball was kicked to you right in front of the goal."

> "Son, I see you got an A-average this quarter, but what happened with this A-minus in advanced trigonometry?"

We're not employers, we're parents. We're not bosses, we're Mom and Dad. Sure, you might feel like "pink slipping" your kid when he messes up, but he's only human. He makes mistakes. Why do you think they invented white correction fluid anyway?

A PARENT'S PERSPECTIVE OF FORGIVENESS

Have you ever caught yourself red-handed in the act of being untruthful with your wife, husband, friend, or boss? How did you wind up in this unenviable position? Were you attempting to portray yourself in a more favorable light? Or were you just trying to save your own skin over some mistake? "Yeah, honey. Sure I remembered our anniversary. Your gift is at my office. I'll just run back and get it. I'll probably do a little work while I'm there so don't expect me for an hour or two."

It's true, certain individuals in your life seem to bring out the worst in you—such as lying. But aren't these the very same people you feel the most *insecure* around? People who are not particularly forgiving of your mistakes. People who remind you of others from your past—like your parents.

How do your children see you? If they view you as a parent who is likely to withhold love should they slip up, then prepare yourself. You may be in for a lifetime's supply of "frequent liar" miles, because your kids will be afraid to tell you the truth.

Many wonderful parts of Scripture deal directly with forgiveness, but the parable about the two debtors (Luke 7:41–43) struck a responsive chord in me. Jesus said to Simon, "Two men owed money to a certain moneylender. One owed him five hundred denarii, and the other fifty. Neither of them had the money to pay him back, so he canceled the debts of both. Now which of them will love him more?" "I suppose the one who had the bigger debt canceled," Simon answered correctly. (Talk about performance under pressure. Way to go, Simon!)

The lesson for parents is that forgiveness is infinitely more powerful than discipline, just as grace is far more positively motivating than truth. A child can more easily admit or "own" his past and present mistakes if he knows that forgiveness (and grace) is waiting on the horizon.

THE GOOD, THE BAD, AND THE UGLY OF A CHILD'S PERSPECTIVE
("I do bad things sometimes, so I must be a bad person.")

From birth onward you should impart two basic, yet critical, lessons to your children: (1) they are human and, as such, are subject to the mistakes of man; (2) your love for them is unconditional and not performance-based.

Children who are raised without proper nurturing, understanding, and love generally end up hopelessly lost down one of two roads. The first road leads to severely narcissistic or grandiose personality traits. These children feel powerful, omnipotent, and in control of their own small world. The second road leads to insecurity and low self-esteem. Either route produces adults who have trouble forming and maintaining close relationships.

Divorce often produces in children symptoms of black-and-white or grandiose thinking. It's not uncommon for a child to believe that he was solely responsible for the breakup of his parents. He may reason, for example, "If I were only a better student . . ." or "if I had done what they told me to do more often . . . Mom and Dad wouldn't have had to yell at me as much. They would have stayed together if I had been better."

Kids sometimes hide behind concrete forms of thinking as a defense against overwhelming feelings of helplessness and vulnerability. If Mom and Dad are happy, it's because they were good. If Mom or Dad is angry, it's because they were bad. Most experts agree that black-and-white thinking begins to grab hold between the ages of three and four, and continues through childhood.[2]

One day a woman brought her ten-year-old son into counseling at the behest of school counselors. Behavioral issues centered around bragging, lying, and acting up. The result of an unplanned and unwanted pregnancy, he had received an absolute minimum amount of attention as a baby. He was changed, bathed, and fed, but virtually starved emotionally.

His mother sadly recalled allowing him to cry for hours until he fell asleep, never once checking to make sure he was all right. She was little more than a caretaker during the first five years of his life—too needy and insecure herself to give the nurturing and love he so desperately needed.

She painfully added that she herself was quick to anger and very strict in her discipline. For example, when her son would accidently break or spill something, he was spanked and sent to his room for several hours. He was able to insulate himself from further pain by becoming grandiose, which made him better, safer, and stronger. Unfortunately, it was a false sense of security that would betray him throughout his formative years.

What a relief, you may be thinking. I don't have to worry about my son needing to insulate himself. While it may be true that you are a loving, caring, and attentive parent, black-and-white thinking in children can occur even in nonabusive, seemingly normal, homes. The difference? Their parents are often overly rigid, controlling, and strict. Yes, they fit the platoon parent mold.

Without professional intervention, the destructive aspects of black-and-white thinking continue into adulthood. If somebody disappoints this type of person—even in the smallest way—he will be perceived as being all bad, even evil. However, if somebody encourages and supports him in a positive way, he will generally idealize that person as being all good, despite being somewhat suspicious.

Black-and-white thinkers have little room in their hearts for forgiveness. If the person they once idealized lets them down even once, their fall from grace is fast—and often irrevocable. It's a vicious circle for children (and adults) who see the world through distorted glasses. The only constants in their lives are disappointment and betrayal. If something good is happening, count on them to sabotage it. Of course, they are only letting down themselves.

How Children and Teenagers Reveal Grandiose Mind-Sets

1. Defensiveness, lying, and insecurity
2. Idealizing others (such as a brother they see as perfect)
3. Perfectionistic tendencies (they must do no wrong or love will be withheld)
4. Depressed (when they've concluded nothing they do will be good enough)
5. Acting up (feels unworthy of love; becomes the black sheep of the family because it's safer than trying to measure up to performance standards)
6. May exaggerate achievements and talents or try to convince others that they are special
7. Reacts defensively to criticism, shame, or humiliation, which is often hidden by anger
8. Believes that he should receive special treatment from parents, teachers, family, and friends

Manipulating Children by Withholding Love

Children, such as those we've discussed, often come from homes where love was dangled like a coupon redeemable only by performing, or where love was virtually nonexistent. Withholding your love—or making it conditional—is not only a good way to alienate your kids but an excellent way to isolate them emotionally from others.

You can restrict a kid to his room, take away his video games and Walkman, but no punishment is more devastating or emotionally damaging than withholding your love. Parents may withhold love when

- ✔ They are unable to resolve their own feelings resulting from a childhood where love was conditional.
- ✔ They use the same rigid standards with their children as they received from their parents. They may also have a false or idealized perception of the success of this parenting style.
- ✔ They fear letting their child know that it's OK to fail, because it may cause them to lose control and their child will stop trying as hard.
- ✔ They selfishly believe that a child who isn't perfect will reflect negatively on them.
- ✔ They may be insecure about themselves and their own parenting style.

Withholding love because your child has failed to "measure up" to your expectations is a cruel communicator. It's like forcing them to wear a large sign emblazoned with the words "I'm not loved. I'm not lovable." These children often carry their emotional battle scars into their own parenting, and so pass this chipped set of china on to their children.

It's vital that you communicate unconditional love and acceptance to your children. Give them a healthy environment where they can be "just good enough kids." Sure they have faults, make mistakes, and get into jams, but they never have to worry about not being loved and appreciated.

NINE KEYS TO BEING A SAFE PARENT

1 *A safe parent creates a safe place for a child to "be himself."* One of the most beautiful things a parent can hear from his child is, "I'm sorry, I messed up." A child or teenager who is able to admit mistakes is telling you that he feels safe in his environment. He knows that he can be himself, which will always be good enough for Mom and Dad.

2 *A safe parent communicates a sense of belonging.* I once spoke with a fourteen-year-old girl who said that she didn't feel a sense of belonging at home. When pressed for details she revealed that her dad disapproved of her choice of friends. He also disliked the fact that she occasionally smoked cigarettes and that she had tried marijuana. Her father overreacted by communicating an emotionally minimizing message that she was less than OK in his eyes. He even told her that she couldn't go to church with the family until her hair was restored to its natural color, which wasn't purple-purple. She had feelings of helplessness, abandonment, isolation, and confusion. After all, wasn't she the same girl she had always been? She realized she shouldn't have tried marijuana or dyed her hair. But how long would her banishment from the family circle last?

Many parents place the blame on their kids. "If they weren't saying and doing such 'bizarre' things, there wouldn't be any problems," parents have told me. The last message you want to communicate to a child or teenager who is acting up is that they are no longer acceptable to you.

3 *A safe parent normalizes weaknesses and makes it OK to be that way.* I've found that one of the most effective ways of normalizing weaknesses in our children is through self-disclosure. This is just as true in a therapeutic setting as it is at home with my own children. My daughter came home after school one day with several math papers that were, quite honestly, horrible. She had obviously inherited my weaknesses—no, wait, complete ineptness—in math.

Some parents feel that admitting to similar shortcomings is like giving their kid a license to fail. I believe in being honest. So I told Tracy that I once supervised NASA's entire computer system. Seriously, I told her I had failed basic math, not once but twice, in junior college. I told her how much begging and pleading it took to convince the dean of students to accept my extra psychology courses in lieu of math credits. She laughed when I told her how he had grown so weary of my whimpering that he allowed me to graduate.

Children need to hear that they aren't alone with their problems. Empathizing, while disclosing your weaknesses in areas similar to theirs, makes you more human and more approachable.

4 *A safe parent normalizes times of sadness and depression, and makes feelings and emotions OK to share.* While conducting a single-parenting seminar, a mom in the back of the room asked, "How can I get my six-year-old to begin talking about the divorce and the loss of his dad? I ask him all the time if he wants to talk about it, but he just says no. The problem is, I know it's bugging him."

Without knowing the family dynamics, I took a shot at the answer by asking the mom if she ever just sits down with her boy and conveys *her* feelings about the divorce. "Do you ever tell him that you have been feeling down, sad, and lonely yourself?" I asked. "No," she answered. "I thought it would make him feel worse if he knew I was sad."

Kids need to hear and see feelings from parents in order to know how to express feelings of their own. Remember, small children are often unable to put their feelings into words. They may tell you they feel sick to their stomachs when they really are just feeling nervous or anxious about a situation. If this mom had sat down with her six-year-old and told him how the divorce had affected her, it would have "freed him up" to disclose his own feelings. He could have identified with her feelings. This would have normalized the way he was feeling, while helping him to feel less insecure about himself and his surroundings.

The same is true of dads. As a kid, I never understood why men didn't cry. It was probably because I never saw my dad cry. I never saw John Wayne cry, either. Both of them were heroes to me. It wasn't until I had kids of my own that I realized how strange it was to be watching a sad movie while trying to fight back the tears. Was this a macho thing or what? Now I cry at movies, weddings, and when the last piece of cheesecake is gone.

5 *A safe parent provides a sense of ownership, and interprets and integrates both good and bad feelings.* Remember, we've talked about the way children tend to see the world—all good or all bad, all black and white. It's up to parents to help kids comprehend the gradations of life—that he can do bad things without being a bad person.

One day my daughter was in one of her rare moods. On the way up the stairs she shouted, "I hate you! You're awful!" *Isn't that special?* I thought. I knew that it was best to think of the incident as an opportunity to discuss her angry feelings. My goal wasn't to talk her out of her angry feelings but rather to let her know it's OK to feel the way she felt without being ashamed. Though no parent enjoys hearing that their child hates him or her, it comes with the territory—just as a mail carrier knows that he's going to be bitten sooner or later.

In chapter 5 we will take a more in-depth look at setting boundaries. For now, keep in mind that our children's feelings fall within their own personal boundaries. We can't request, demand, or sanction them into feeling differently.

6 *A safe parent gives permission to tell the truth even when it will disappoint.* How many of us will tell the truth to a spouse, even when it will hurt? Husbands, when was the last time you told your wife that you thought her latest hairdo looked like a cross between Elvira, Mistress of the Dark, and Lassie? Never, unless you were having suicidal tendencies that day. And wives, when was the last time you told your husband that he could stand to lose a few pounds? OK, so that was a bad example.

Children need to learn the scriptural significance of telling the truth: "You will know the truth, and the truth will set you free" (John 8:32). This is one of life's truly imperative lessons that must be communicated to your children. Telling the truth has an emotionally cleansing affect on the conscience. Take into consideration how difficult it can be for a child or teenager to admit they've done something wrong before you automatically condemn them for a mess up. I'm not saying to grant them amnesty for merely telling the truth. If there are to be consequences, so be it. But don't forget to celebrate the honesty of his act. The fact that he was able to come forward with the truth, though it meant certain punishment, is a significant event that shouldn't be lost behind the dastardly deed.

7 *A safe parent provides an environment where kids see themselves as individuals, separate from their parents.* Genesis 2:24 explains God's plan for us to leave our parents and to "cleave" to a husband or wife in a mature relationship. At an appropriate time in our children's emotional development, they need to see and understand their separateness from us. For most, the "leaving process" begins in the stages of "separation-individuation" in early childhood. For others, this process is never allowed to proceed normally. These children have difficulty maintaining mature relationships as adults because they weren't afforded any freedom to grow and individualize.

What types of parenting styles lead to the alienation of children in this sense? Parents who are enmeshed (fused emotionally) with their children and don't give them the psychological freedom to leave the nest, and overly controlling parents who don't allow their kids the freedom they need to mature emotionally and develop greater independence. Don't be afraid to let your kids grow up. Trust in it; it's God's plan.

8 *A safe parent enables a child to make better decisions because fear and performance standards don't dominate the thought process.* I once spoke with a teenager who was having trouble making decisions. He was unsure of the classes he wanted in college. He couldn't decide if he should live in the dorm or at home. He couldn't decide if he should buy a used car or dip into his savings for a new car. Essentially, he said he couldn't make any decisions for himself. The side effect of his indecisiveness was anxiety, since he knew the day was fast approaching when he would have to become more independent.

When we began taking a closer look into his childhood the answer was evident. His father (a platoon parent if ever there was one) made most of the decisions for all of the children. The few times he recalled being able to make an independent decision, he remarked knowing that "it had better be the right one or there would be an endless stream of reminders and I-told-you-so's." The insecure reminders of a less than fulfilling, dependent childhood prevented this young man from making his own decisions. Through therapy, we were able to work past his fear of failure, which had been fostered by the constant worry over disappointing his father.

If your kids make a mistake, help them to see it, own it, correct it, and then move on. After all, much of life is learned by trial and error.

9 *A safe parent teaches that there are consequences for their kids' actions (reaping and sowing).* Little is as foundational to a balanced life as the relationship between reaping and sowing, cause and effect. We begin communicating these principles to our children at a very young age. It's the pushover parent who usually has the most problems with the principle of reaping and sowing.

If you're a pushover parent, you know what I'm talking about. How many times can you recall making the statement, "If you don't eat your vegetables, you won't get any dessert." In families where

the reaping and sowing principle has teeth, follow-through is com-
monplace—no veggies, no cake. In families where the pushover parent reigns, the child manages to escape the salad bar and goes
directly to the dessert tables. In addition to being highly manipulative, the child has also learned to "play off" his parent's desire to be a
friend instead of a parent.

This message becomes more clear to these children as they
mature. What started out as a simple manipulation in the hopes of
scoring some chocolate cake has blossomed into a full-fledged avoid-
ance problem. Absent is the foundation of reaping and sowing, which
allows us to take responsibility for our mistakes.

PICK 'EM UP, DUST 'EM OFF,
AND LOVE 'EM UNCONDITIONALLY

We're terrific at keeping our kids fed and warm at night. We
make sure they have nice clothes for school and church. We keep
them in toys and video games. And should even the smallest space
appear between pearly whites, we break the budget for braces. All
too often, though, we lose sight of where our responsibilities to our
children begin and end. Simply being a caretaker parent isn't enough
—in fact, it's far too much. Kids who come from caretaker homes
don't take responsibility for their actions. Why should they?

Caretaker parents are usually aggressive and somewhat overbearing. It's hardly a coincidence that their children tend to be passive
and manipulative. An event such as a severe childhood illness that
leaves an infant weak and vulnerable often triggers the caretaking process.

Timmy and Linda are a classic example of how the caretaking
cycle begins and where it leads. Timmy was born prematurely and
was not expected to survive his first few days on this earth. Through
the grace of God, however, he managed to pull through. Although he
was allowed to go home after three weeks of intensive care, he had
significant health problems over the next several years. During that
time, his mom, Linda, remained home and tirelessly met his every
need. She even made a bed for Timmy in their room, where he slept
until he was seven. If he so much as coughed, Linda kept him out of
school. If he wanted a hamburger for dinner instead of what the rest
of the family was having, she immediately jumped in her car and sped
off to McDonalds.

Let's check in on Timmy during his high school years. At fifteen, he started to rebel a little against his mom's caretaking style, but not to the point of jeopardizing a good thing. He learned that displays of anger, for example, would cause her to work even harder to please him. He had become a world-class manipulator. If he was tired of doing homework, he might throw a pencil across the room to punctuate his frustration—all for Mom's benefit, of course. And she would come to the rescue, asking, "Can I help you with that, honey?" She would invariably finish his homework.

She was devastated when Timmy went away to college. She would call him daily without regard to the mounting long-distance charges. He had only to hint about money, and Mom would quickly wire him the money he needed to finance his burgeoning social activities, which were becoming a strain on the family's budget. Too little studying, too many parties, and Timmy was bounced from the university. As you have probably already guessed, he was welcomed back home with open arms.

Timmy decided he needed "space"—time to relax from the rigors of higher education. He never worked or offered to help around the house. When Timmy's father suggested that he ought to be doing something with his life, such as other schooling options, Linda sprang to his defense: "Timmy just needs a little time, that's all."

When Timmy was arrested for drunk driving, Mom bailed him out. She went with him to court. She signed him up for his court-appointed educational classes. If she could have taken the "rap" for him, she would have. In actuality, Linda was never satisfied just being a mom. She aspired to be the *perfect* mom. If that meant doing everything for her son, fine.

Timmy's caretaking mom carried everything to extremes. How willing are *your* kids to assume accountability for their actions? My daughter once lost the magazine subscription order forms that she had received from school. She was naturally worried about the consequences of her carelessness. After much wailing and fretting, her mom said she would accompany Tracy to class and explain things to the teacher.

"Time out," I reminded her. "That's a caretaking misdemeanor." She agreed. Tracy should be allowed to accept responsibility for her actions by telling the teacher herself. By the way, kids feel a sense of pride and accomplishment when they handle their own problems. As a general rule, parents should give only the minimum amount of help necessary to solve the problem.

As parents, we should see ourselves as shepherds tending our flock. We are called to keep our flock safe, on course, moving in the right direction. Many parents tend their flock by picking up and carrying their lambs until they grow weary under the pressure. They put the lamb down, rest a bit, and then carry it some more. This is a very fatiguing method of parenting, one that never allows the lamb to grow stronger.

"VE HAVE VAYS OF MAKING YOU TALK . . ."

Parents who set stringent performance standards for their kids often dispense love with a truckload of conditions attached. Their children must qualify for love and respect by meeting a set of standards. When a child does good (in the eyes of the parent), they receive a small ration of love and praise for that deed only. One little mess-up and all love might be yanked away. Keeping your children on a strict performance value system has detrimental side effects:

- ✔ Serious insecurity, since the child is always measuring her value and successes based on reaction from parents and others
- ✔ Resentment of authority
- ✔ Rebelliousness or impulsive behavior
- ✔ Constant approval-seeking
- ✔ Being immobilized by fears of failure

THE DREADED LITTLE-LEAGUE PARENT

Who among us haven't witnessed the dreaded little-league parent in action? They are either cursing at umpires or grousing because their kid is playing right field instead of pitching. "The coach is a moron," they might whisper under their breath.

On one particular Saturday morning at Tracy's soccer field, the art of little-league parenthood reached new levels of absurdity. I was standing on the sidelines offering encouragement to my daughter when I was approached by a small group of parents (they looked a little like a lynch mob) armed with fistfuls of dollar bills.

"Hi, Greg. How about kicking in a couple of bucks for the new scoring pool we just started?"

"Sorry?" I asked in astonishment.

"You're a shrink; you'll love the concept," the leader of the pack chimed in. "Every time one of our kids scores a goal, they get a buck. A buck a goal. Pretty good incentive, huh?"

"Sorry, guys. I don't think this is a particularly good idea," I said. "We would be putting them on a performance standard that offers rewards for meeting our own personal expectations and by-passes the reason they're out here anyway—sportsmanship, cama-raderie, and exercise. Besides, *your* kids would end up with all my money. No, on the contrary, they should feel equally good about themselves whether they win, lose, score goals, or get shut out."

My words fell on deaf ears as they marched away grumbling something about psychologists. I don't know if there was any con-nection, but my name was conspicuously absent from the post-sea-son barbecue/swim party invitation list.

DISAPPOINTMENT AND WITHHOLDING LOVE
("I'm not OK . . . you're not OK . . . but that's OK.")

While conducting a radio interview I received a classic call deal-ing with parents who withhold love because of disappointment. The conversation went something like this:

MOM: "What should we do? My seventeen-year-old daughter, Melissa, came home last week and told my husband and me that she is pregnant. We are devastated. We thought we had instilled proper values. We don't know if we should insist that the boy marry her or get out of our lives. How are we going to be able to show our faces at church once the news gets out?"

ME: "Wait just a minute," I interrupted. "Is your daughter home right now?"

MOM: "Yes. She's listening in the other room."

ME: "Fine. Put her on the phone."

A moment later, the daughter picked up the phone with a sheepish, "Hello, Doctor."

ME: "Hi, Melissa. Having a difficult time, huh, kiddo?"

MELISSA: "Yeah, I guess we are."

ME: "Who's we?"
MELISSA: "My mom and dad and me."
ME: "How have your parents acted toward you since you broke the news to them?"
MELISSA: "Well, they've been angry. My dad won't really talk to me, and my mom just worries about what the ladies from her Bible study are going to think."
ME: "Do you feel loved and wanted right now, at this moment?"
MELISSA: "No. I think I just ruined everybody's life."

Let's say for a moment that you're Melissa's parent. What would be your first response to the news?

A. "How will our friends at church accept us after this?"
B. "Should I send her away to another school?"
C. "How best can we help our daughter?"
D. "How do we keep this a secret?"
E. "Where did we go wrong?"
F. All of the above

As well-balanced parents, you obviously selected "C." *Big deal*, you might be thinking, *any parent would have made the proper selection.* However, you would be surprised to learn that many parents become so caught up in their own expectations and disappointments that they miss the point: "What can we do for our daughter?"

At no point during our conversation did "Mom" express concern for her daughter's feelings. Instead, she focused on her own projections of disappointment and embarrassment should the pregnancy become public. Was she willing to withhold love from her daughter if the situation wasn't resolved to her satisfaction? Quite possibly.

Fortunately for Melissa, we were able to connect her with an excellent teen pregnancy support group. She also received some short-term family counseling, which helped everyone concerned sort through their feelings.

True, it's natural for all of us to experience fleeting feelings of embarrassment, or even shame, when our kids mess up. There are ample opportunities for both emotions during the rearing of children.

The real question to ask yourself is, "How is God going to judge our actions—as honorable or self-centered?" What if your kid got caught shoplifting or cheating on an exam in school? In varying degrees, most of us would care about how we were judged by others. However, selfish interests should never obstruct our ability to parent in a well-balanced manner. Working through a parent's feelings of disappointment is often the first order of business in family therapy, even before the child's behavioral problems can be tackled.

IF IT'S BROKE, FIX IT!

Some people spend countless hours restoring classic automobiles. They pour themselves into a project with all their heart. They painstakingly return every bolt, bumper, and door handle to its original luster. If, in the process, a headlight should suddenly break, they don't junk the entire project—they fix it. I believe that kids deserve the same attention.

I met with the parents of a sixteen-year-old who was continually in trouble. In one year, he had gone from being a solid B-student to D's and failing grades. He frequently defied boundaries and rules and was "foul mouthed" toward his parents. After nearly getting into a physical confrontation with his father over a mishap with the family car, his parents called my office. They were looking for referrals to a year-round boys camp or boarding school.

If your children have a problem, help them fix it. Only under the most severe circumstances does sending them away or admitting them to a psychiatric hospital program make therapeutic sense. These extreme measures are often pursued in order to relieve the parent's own frustrations, shame, and embarrassment. It is the human equivalent of dumping your car because the ashtray is full.

HOME SHOULD BE A SAFE PLACE TO FAIL

Let your kids know that home is not only where the weeds need to be pulled, it is also a safe place to land—a welcomed port in a storm when navigating gets tough.

I'll never forget the surprise that greeted me one evening as I was pulling into our driveway. Illuminated by my car's headlights was a two-foot tall metallic silver letter *T*. Not an entire word, just the letter T—must have taken half a can of spray paint, too. In disbelief,

I slowly approached the door with the same incredulous feeling usually reserved for wayward lizards that have the nerve to perch on my living room sofa.

"Who in the world would do this to my precious garage door?" As an ex-detective I quickly ran through my list of the most obvious suspects. My son? No, why would he write a T on the door, unless of course he was trying to frame someone whose name actually begins with T, like . . . like . . . TRACY.

I tracked the fashion princess through the house following a trail of Oreo cookie crumbs until I found her sharpening her shopping skills by perusing the most recent Toys-R-Us catalog. "Hello, Tracy, and how was your day today?" I asked. "Anything interesting happen?"

"Nope, Daddy. How was your day?" she replied sweetly.

"Oh, it was just lovely until I pulled into the driveway and noticed we've redecorated. Any idea what I'm talking about?"

Ever notice how children can look you straight in the eye and say nothing for minutes at a time? It becomes a "stare out" of sorts. They know, I'm sure, that you are lots older then they are and, if they can wait you out long enough, you'll die first.

"No, what's 'redecorated,' Daddy?" Yeah, right! Play innocent with old Dr. Daddy, will you? I've a reputation to uphold.

"Why don't you come with me to the front yard, and I'll show you what I mean dearest daughter, apple of my eye." She walked outside and stood directly in front of the big T without my having to point it out—curious. "Have any idea who the artist is?"

"Nope," she replied.

"You sure?" I inquired.

"It wasn't me, Daddy."

I quickly slipped into the Columbo mode and asked her, "Gee, can you think of anybody around here whose name begins with the letter T?"

"Me?" she said sheepishly. "But I didn't do it, Dad. I wasn't even here today."

Note to parents: You've got your kids "dead to rights" when they start alibiing about never having been at the "scene of the crime."

"I'll tell you what, Tracy," I said in my most sincere "Father Knows Best" understanding voice. "I'm not really so upset about the

T on my garage door. We all make mistakes, and they can always be fixed. What I want you to think about is telling the truth. I'll never be angry with you for making mistakes, but there are always going to be consequences for lying."

After a few moments of thinking over the options, she decided to come clean. "I wrote the letter T. I'm sorry I did it." As her punishment, Tracy was ordered to don heavy, yellow gloves and use multiple toxic chemicals to scrub off her handiwork. The door looked fine, and we used my daughter as a night light for days.

If your kids don't feel safe to confide in you when they mess up something small—like writing an initial on the house—how do you expect them to come to you when they are really in trouble?

A FINAL THOUGHT ON BEING A SAFE PARENT

The old fifties TV series "Leave It to Beaver" has been much maligned and satirized over the years. But, you know, old Ward Cleaver created a safe environment for his kids. He very seldom lost his temper, although you could always tell when he was angry about something. He was firm but fair. He laid down a set of reasonable boundaries for his kids. Above all, he never withheld love when they messed up.

The "Bill Cosby Show" of the nineties also featured a good parenting model of providing a safe emotional haven for kids. He communicated that you don't have to be perfect—"I still love you," and, "If you mess up, I'll help you fix it."

I feel strongly that kids should know that nothing is permanently broken. After all, that's why we have spackle, Super Glue, and wood putty. The world hasn't come to an end when they've messed up. And while there may be consequences for their actions, they will always be loved.

As a kid growing up, I remember my mom constantly working and reworking her oil paintings. A professional artist, she often said that any mistake could be corrected as long as the oils hadn't dried. Parents, too, have the opportunity to catch their mistakes and make corrections early in a kid's development, long before any problems become permanent.

4

If You Really Want to Alienate Your Kids . . .
DON'T WORRY
ABOUT QUALITY TIME

While driving down a long stretch of highway on an early morning commute, you become aware of a slight drift to the left. You compensate by nudging the steering wheel to the right, but it only forestalls the inevitable. Finally, after your minivan nearly dances across a medium strip, you have no alternative but to visit the local garage. My wife calls it "the morgue"—the place where our cars go to die. She's certain the repair bill will rival the national debt, but it's nothing terminal this time, only tires badly in need of balancing.

My wife has a unique perspective about automotive problems. When one of those pesky little "idiot lights" on her dashboard starts flashing "CHECK OIL," most people would check the oil, right? My wife simply tapes one of my son's baseball cards over the light so it won't bother her anymore. I discover the problem only after the plastic around the CHECK OIL light has suffered a major meltdown from the heat. Worse, it has scorched the back of Nolan Ryan's head. "Honey, please! Promise me that if this ever happens again, you'll never use a Nolan Ryan card. That's what 'manager cards' are for."

PARENTING PIT STOPS

People, too, can find themselves drifting off course for no apparent reason. That's when it's advisable to ease off the gas pedal and coast in for a well-deserved "parenting pit stop." Call it preventative maintenance for the soul.

How might a routine service check begin? First of all, get yourself a clipboard. All experienced "service writers" have clipboards. Next, pencil in a two-column check list of the current priorities in your life. In one column, list only the most *important* things in your life. In the other, jot down only the *essential* things. Highlight any item that you suspect may be out of balance, showing wear, or in need of a major overhaul.

The following model will undoubtably differ from yours, but the goal remains the same—to strike a balance between the important and essential things in your life.

Important	Essential
making more money	your relationship with Jesus
getting ahead in business	significant fellowship
hobbies/recreation	quality time with your spouse
spending time with friends	quality time with your kids
having fun/playing	quality time as a family
exercise	
acquiring property/things	

If your inspection reveals that you are placing too much emphasis on the *important,* rather than the *essential,* things in your life, pull into the first service bay, leave the keys, and ask yourself the following questions:

1 *Have my priorities changed or shifted?* Am I paying too much attention to the important things and not enough to the essential things? (Save your notes for future use. This exercise should be considered

routine maintenance. Your answers will provide you with a clear service record.)

2 *If my priorities have changed, what happened?* How did I become preoccupied with the less essential things? There are always traceable reasons for a life that's tilting out of balance. Perhaps it's because you find it difficult to set limits and boundaries. You may find it hard to say no to friends, bosses, and others who continually want and expect more from you. There may have been financial pressures that drove you to work twelve-hour days. Or maybe you just have a "Type A" driven personality. Or, possibly, your parents lived their lives out of balance, and you've adopted those standards.

3 *Have I lost sight of my priorities altogether?* Have you ever ridden a roller coaster as it rumbles through a long, pitch-black tunnel? It's an unnerving feeling, isn't it? You feel helpless and out of control. You know there are going to be tremendous peaks, major valleys, and hairpin turns ahead, but you can't see or anticipate them. A severely out-of-balance life is much like an emotional roller coaster ride in the dark. You find yourself strapped in, going along for the ride, unable to anticipate changes, and powerless to make corrections.

A FIVE-POINT CHECK UP

After you've determined that your priorities are, in fact, out of balance, I suggest you authorize repair immediately. It could help you avoid more costly repair bills down the road. The most effective way to begin this process is to sit down and reprioritize your life. As the greasy, grimy auto mechanic used to say in those motor oil commercials, "You can pay me now or pay me later."

The following biblically based check list has proved extremely useful in my life, especially when my own priorities seem to be shifting in one direction or another. How does it compare with yours? Remember, it should be used as a starting place only. Your own priority check list will require honesty, commitment, and prayer to establish and maintain.

1. My relationship with God
2. My relationship with my wife
3. My relationship with my children

4. My ministry (my patients' well-being, writing books, public speaking, doing radio shows)
5. My job (administrative duties at the clinic)

AN OUT-OF-BALANCE LIFE

A friend of mine from my police days called and left a rather distressing message on my answering machine: "Greg, I'm in trouble! My marriage is on the rocks, and Meg told me that she's going to leave if I don't get some help right away."

When I called back I learned that he and his wife, both wonderful Christian people who had been married for more than eight years, were teetering on the brink of separation or divorce. "Tell me what's going on, Rick."

"I guess I've been going through life with blinders on or something," he said. "Ever since I took the promotion to detective, she tells me I've changed. She says I've been ignoring her and the kids. She even said she's thought about having an affair with some guy she works with. Can you believe it? She told me if I don't figure out what's wrong with my life fast, she's taking off with the kids. What can I do?"

I met with my old friend over coffee (minus the donuts) and began helping him investigate the root causes behind his marital crisis. I asked him what a typical work week looked like for him.

"Well, I work the normal five days a week in the robbery division. My hours are 8:30 A.M. to about 6:30 P.M. weekdays," he said.

"What about your evenings and weekends?"

"Well, on Monday and Wednesday nights I go to school. On Tuesday I attend the evening Bible study at my church. On Thursday I'm home for dinner, and on Friday I go out with the guys and play poker or shoot pool," he said.

"What about your weekends?" I asked.

"On Saturday mornings, I play softball with the police team and then I come home and do the yard work. On Sundays we go to morning service, come home, and I usually watch TV or read the paper. Then we might all go out to dinner together or visit my folks."

The situation was clear. My friend had fallen into a very common priority pit—one that get's deeper and more difficult to escape from with time. Work wasn't Rick's problem. It was all of the extracurricular activities in his life. If we're not careful, those extra commitments just seem to accumulate, like boxes of stuff in the garage, and we're never sure how they got there—we just know they're stacked everywhere.

We start out with a reasonably clean itinerary. We decide to attend Bible study or join the choir practice, but that's only one or two nights a week. Then reality sinks in. If we really want to get ahead at work, we may have to return to school to get a college degree. There goes another two or three nights. Then peer group pressures mount, and we agree to go out with the boys one night a week. (Under the guise of rest and relaxation.) Then someone at work, usually your boss, wants you to join the company bowling or softball team. You can't let the boss down, now can you? The next thing you know, your life is completely out of balance.

It was time for Rick to sit down with Meg and determine what she really wanted and needed from him. After some marriage counseling (with a colleague of mine), the couple became more open and honest about their individual needs. At last check, they were doing much better.

Ladies, be forewarned—your lives can also be pushed severely out of alignment. Between juggling a career, a family, the women's Bible study, aerobics, Girl Scout leading, soccer practice, car pooling, it's easy to see that guys don't have a corner on the priority pit stop market.

Many people, especially those of us who grew up in the so-called "me first generation" (the fifties), forget to set and maintain priorities. Frequent pit stops to check for emotional wear and tear is an integral part of keeping our lives well tuned.

What does leading a properly prioritized life have to do with being a good parent? If you are living a balanced life, you are probably enjoying the fruits of success and happiness. If you are seriously out of balance, you're probably modeling a dysfunctional lifestyle for your children. And you are probably not feeling spiritually, relationally, or personally fulfilled.

TAKING CARE OF "NO. 1" DOESN'T MEAN *YOU* ANYMORE

Selfishness is the most common symptom associated with out-of-balance parents. Remember when you were single? Come on, it wasn't that long ago. If you wanted to go to the movies, you went. If you wanted to sleep until noon, you slept. I remember when my brother was single—he actually kept his fishing worms in the produce crisper of his refrigerator. He's married now, and the worms are burrowing under his lawn where they belong. As a single person, your job was easy—you had the luxury of tending exclusively to your own needs and wishes.

As husbands, wives, moms, and dads our lives have changed—no doubt for the better. We have people who depend on us for love and support—who in turn give us love and support. It's a wonderful arrangement. It's only when we slip into selfish behavioral modes that our priorities become blurred, our lives out of balance. I'm not saying we shouldn't care for ourselves, but do so in concert with the wishes of God and the needs of family.

If your children grow up in an environment where meaningful priorities are ignored in favor of selfish pursuits—work over kids, Monday Night Football over spouse—it will be far more difficult for them to keep their own priorities in perspective. Be positive role models. Give your kids the necessary road maps in the form of priorities steeped in God's word. Give them balance.

A DEVOTED AND BALANCED LIFE

1 *Devoting time for regular worship.* A truly balanced life is only attainable through a committed, personal relationship with Jesus Christ. For most people this means daily prayer, weekly church attendance, and regular fellowship.

2 *Devoting time to be with your mate.* Good partners usually make good parents. They're team players, such as Gilligan and the Skipper, Gomez and Morticia. Schedule and guard the precious times you have together. This could include a once a week date night, quiet times, and daily prayer.

3 *Devoting quality time to be with your children.* We'll be discussing quality time in greater detail later, but, for now, start with the understanding that your children need frequent periods of undivided love and attention.

4 *Devoting time for yourself.* "Man does not live by work alone." Or how about "All work and no play makes parents really cranky people"? It's true. A balanced life includes time with friends, exercise, recreation, hobbies, and just plain having fun.

5 *Avoiding devotion to a career.* Work is important. But keep things in balance. I work for two very basic reasons. First, so that I can help others by utilizing the gifts God gave me. And second, to provide for my family so that we may enjoy a more abundant life. Sometimes it takes hard work to maintain that perspective.

For some dads, self-worth is measured by their success on the job. While there's nothing inherently wrong with ambition and hard work—indeed, little is accomplished without it—try to keep your job in perspective and your priorities clear. Don't be so preoccupied with climbing the corporate ladder that you fail to notice your relationships eroding at home. Remember, no man on his death bed was ever overheard saying, "I wish I had spent more time at work." Don't loose sight of the fact that true success is measured by your Christian faith and values, your relationship with the Lord, and your role as a husband and father.

As families with two working parents become more prevalent, many women report allowing their identities and priorities to become just as wrapped-up in work as their husbands. In addition, they have other handicaps that men don't commonly have, such as overcoming stereotypes, competing for fewer jobs, and working similar jobs as men but for less pay.

QUALITY TIME OR QUANTITY TIME —WHAT'S THE DIFFERENCE? (I hate Barbies. I love Nintendo.)

There's no point in sugar-coating this one—I dislike Barbie dolls. They have no redeeming value other than the considerable enjoyment they provide my daughter. Did I say "dislike"? I meant to say, "I hate Barbies!" I feel better now.

I hate the fact that Barbie has five thousand outfits, and my daughter wants every one of them. I hate knowing that she drives a Corvette. And I hate all of her little friends. Especially Ken—he's got a Corvette, too.

But I love Nintendo. It's just plain fun. There's plenty of action. For me, it's baseball, football, and hockey rolled into one. Best of all, my son loves Nintendo, too. You're probably not surprised to learn that my daughter hates Nintendo. My son, of course, hates Barbie. Don't you wish everything in life was that clear?

Here's my dilemma. If I never play Barbie with my daughter, only Nintendo with my son, what am I really saying? I'm discounting the things she enjoys doing. Worse, I'm telling her that her interests are less important than those of my son. (I have this recurring nightmare, that Nintendo will introduce a Barbie game and I'll end up with an aversion to Nintendo as well.)

As a well-balanced parent always in training, my job is to slice quality as evenly as possible between my kids. If that means playing Barbie, I'll play Barbie—even if that means racing her little red Corvette across the carpet while fighting back an almost uncontrollable urge to crash it into a wall. "Sorry, honey. Barbie had an awful accident. I'm afraid she's in the hospital for the rest of the week. The car? Mr. Goodwrench says it will take at least a decade to get it running again."

I must confess, however, to having a different set of rules connected with playing Barbie.

MY BARBIE RULES

1. There must be absolutely no chance of being discovered by a friend, relative, or even the meter reader.
2. The doors must be locked, dead-bolted, and all shades drawn.
3. If someone should penetrate this defense, they must be silenced or forced to eat my wife's meat loaf. Most would choose to be silenced.

HER BARBIE RULES

1. I must get down at carpet level and play Barbie the way she likes to play.
2. I must be Ken and only Ken. (Trust me, I've attempted being G.I. Joe, who has just been hired as Barbie's bodyguard—no dice.)
3. I must always marry Barbie. And I must hum the wedding song as the handsome plastic couple strolls down the isle.
4. I may not use excuses to get out of marrying Barbie, such as Ken is too tired from his bachelor party or he has an ingrown toenail or the wedding is postponed until after the football game.

After the wedding I'm free to play Nintendo.

Fast-Forward Ten Years

My daughter, now eighteen, is reminiscing about her childhood when she bursts into laughter and says, "You know, Dad, I never really cared for playing Barbie when I was a little kid—I just played because I knew you liked it."

I believe that fifteen minutes of quality time is worth at least one hour of quantity time. And that doesn't mean sitting on the couch and watching reruns of Gilligan's Island. Although the episode when Gilligan finds a monkey and . . . never mind.

Quality time is becoming an active participant with your children, not some couch potato sitting on the sidelines watching TV—the ultimate of passive activities. Watching TV with your children is OK, but it's merely passing time. An exception would be selecting programs with a significant message or topic to discuss with your children. Good luck.

The Bottom Line Is Quality Time

Keep track of the quality time you spend with your children, especially if you have a multiple-kid family. Keeping a mental ledger allows you to better balance your time equally among your children. Otherwise, you could end up with eight hours of Nintendo versus eight minutes of Barbie.

Get the most out of quality time by including the whole gang whenever possible—whether or not the activity is universally loved. My daughter, for example, enjoys board games (they should have spelled them "bored games" if you ask me). My son doesn't. No matter, he still gets a sincere invitation to join us. He may not be thrilled at the prospect, but he is obviously pleased about having been asked.

The same holds true when I'm playing Nintendo with my son. Although my daughter doesn't participate, she enjoys spectating from the best seat in the house—my lap. She understands that she has a standing invitation to join in any time she likes.

Toys, Creativity, and the "Gimmies"

The gimmies are thoughts, feelings, and wishes verbalized when your kids want something. It usually starts off with "Paleeeaaassseee" and ends with "That's not fair." The gimmies, like a metal detector over a chunk of iron, become loudest when you're within a hundred feet of any toy aisle. The gimmie alarm also sounds when kids are bored or have just watched three hours worth of toy commercials. When my kids come down with a severe case of the gimmies, I feel like hanging a sign around their little necks that reads, "Please don't feed the Gimmies."

I have found toys to be among the most efficient quality time killers known to man. Some toys are capable of isolating children physically and emotionally, while others simply stagnate their minds through sheer boredom. But take heart. I've stumbled upon a simple formula for beating the gimmies—arts and crafts.

A while back, my wife sent (I should say banished) me and the kids to the neighborhood arts and crafts store for some hot glue sticks. Hot glue sticks? Whatever happened to Elmer's Glue-All or that white paste that some kid named Bret was always eating in every third-grade class around the country?

To my surprise, our little glue stick excursion also introduced my kids to the world of arts and crafts. They were fascinated by the many art projects on display—from wooden airplane kits to "puff paint" T-shirts. They were anxious to try them all. We soon began spending more time in the balsa wood aisle than we did at the toy store.

Now when I see the gimmies coming, we jump in the car and head for the craft store for modeling clay, glider kits, puff paints, or whatever is new. Best of all, helping them with their projects is a tremendous opportunity for quality time. Be sure, though, that your kids don't use the hot glue gun to try to stick the dog to the floor.

A Basic Rule of Quality Time

We should set the record straight now. Quality time seldom (if ever) involves an activity that you actually enjoy doing. For me, playing Barbie is a perfect example. Quality time should revolve around your children's special interests and desires. For my daughter, that means Barbie dolls, drawing, reading, going to the park or to the mall, or just a trip to the market for a gallon of milk. Look for any opportunity to be alone together. For my son, quality time with Dad is tossing a football, playing baseball, kicking a soccer ball, shooting baskets, drawing, playing army men or ninja turtles, and going to the park.

Try penciling in a simple "laundry list" of your children's current hobbies and interests. Chances are you'll notice a number of crossover items. I can maximize quality time with my kids, for example, by drawing pictures with them and going to the park. This technique should not be used to replace individual time, only enhance the relationships you have with your children.

An effective way of compiling a quality time list is to ask your kids what they enjoy doing as a family. Be prepared. The things you thought they enjoyed probably went out six months or a year ago. Try to stay current with their interests or they will not look forward to quality time.

Making Dates with Your Kids (Alone Time)

How is it possible to carve out more quality time in the frenzied nineties? My advice is to make a date with your kids. Once the date is set, be sure you keep it. I believe that quality time needs to be scheduled or it will get lost in our never-ending list of "things to do." Ideally, attempt to set aside an hour or two of individual time with your children every week.

That may *sound* easy, but scheduling "alone time" can get to be quite a challenge. If you have two or more kids, you'll need to be extra creative with your time. You might try a revolving date system that includes a different child weekly. Some families have also had success when Mom takes one child out on a date, while Dad takes the other. Above all, don't underestimate the value of spending time alone with your kids.

How much time constitutes quality time? Is it an all-day thing? Half a day or a few hours? The answer is all of the above. It's far more important to focus on the quality rather than on specific lengths of time.

Quality Time Is an Investment in Their Future

I have one friend who hasn't missed a week of scheduled quality time with her teenagers in four years. This is obviously a woman who enjoys the relationships she has established with her children, which are continually strengthened and reinforced by the quality time she spends with them. If you're thinking, *How can I afford to make that kind of commitment of time every week?* may I remind you that you really can't afford not to?

As a parent, I was curious to know how she had accomplished this enviable record of quality time. "There are some weeks when it's pretty difficult, and I have to be a little creative," she said. "After dropping my son off at soccer practice, I might take my daughter to the coffee shop where we can share some quality time. My son is another story. Since he's so busy at school with various sports, I might make a breakfast or lunch date with him for the weekend. The amazing part about our quality time is that, even if it's only an hour a week, it makes a difference. It's an investment in their futures."

The real litmus test of quality time comes after the fact: Will your kids remember those golden moments tomorrow, next week, or—in some cases—the rest of their lives? How many quality times do *you* remember from *your* childhood?

STARTING A QUALITY TIME PROGRAM

Some parents have asked me at what age they should begin to spend quality time with their children. How about today? The earlier you begin scheduling quality time in your child's life the better. I'm not saying purchase a megaphone and start jabbering at your child while he's still in the womb. Wait until birth, but don't feel like you've missed the boat if you haven't considered quality time until now. Quality time can begin at any age with tremendous results.

If you are interested in beginning a quality time program with your older children or teenagers, I suggest the following:

  ✔ Let them know why you are interested in quality time. (You enjoy spending time with them and you see this as an opportunity for the two of you to get closer.)
  ✔ Explain the program to them and ask them what they think of the idea.
  ✔ Ask them what types of things they would enjoy doing during quality time.

✔ Let them know that you will respect their time, wants, and wishes.

✔ Post a family calendar with quality time blocked out each week. When scheduling time with your children, ask them if they are free on that particular day. Ask them what they might like to do while you're together. This will help them to feel more invested in the quality time process.

We're Having Quality Time, and You'll Like It!

You can lead a child to water, but you can't make him wash his hands. And you can't force your child to have the time of his life with you.

Quality time should be considerate. It's important to respect your kids' free time and the activities they enjoy, especially with older children. Begin with an understanding that most older children, and especially teenagers, would rather spend dull, lousy, wasted hours with their friends than ten quality minutes with their parents. Actually, many parents would rather have a root canal (on a good tooth) than struggle for topics of conversation with a teenager. If you are forcing your children to conform to your concept of quality time, you're probably taking a significant step toward alienating them.

Screaming Hormones, Quality Time, and Your Teenager

Those of you with teenagers might be thinking, *Right, my teenager doesn't even publicly acknowledge that he has parents. He doesn't want to go on family outings. He doesn't want to be seen at church in our company. He even ducks down in the car should we pass somebody we know. How can I get him to start spending quality time with me?*

As your children mature, they will enter a difficult stage of development between the ages of twelve and fourteen—you know, that period in a youngster's life when his parents become more difficult. In developmental terms, you can compare this period to stages your child went through at twenty-four-months of age. Remember when your child embarked on a real "power trip"? He discovered the word *no* and began to define and express his own personality. Many developmental experts agree that somewhere around puberty teenagers go through a second phase of separation/individuation. During this phase they may not want to hang around home or even be seen with their parents.

When starting a quality time program with your teenager expect resistance. Be prepared to talk this through. Follow the steps described in the quality time program and ask if they would agree to give it a thirty-day trial period. (Teenagers find it easier to accept uncomfortable things if they think it's not going to be forever.)

If you know what activities your teen would enjoy doing, you have a head start in planning your quality time dates. A date might even include buying them something, such as breakfast or a new pair of jeans—anything to help them see that quality time doesn't have to be painful or boring. It may seem like bribery (I guess it actually is), but you've got to begin some place.

Little Things May Mean a Lot

Don't overlook those seemingly insignificant little things that mean so much to our children. For example, both my kids love to draw. Naturally, these art projects are often presented to Mom and Dad as gifts. This is a tremendous opportunity for a quality moment—don't let it slip away. Make an appropriately big deal out of their special projects. If you only glance at it and say "That's nice, honey," you're sending a minimizing message.

I'm not saying to hustle out and have every finger painting professionally mounted and framed with museum lighting, but give the creation a sufficient amount of praise. We all know how sensitive artists can be, so provide Picasso with a place of honor for his work—the refrigerator will do nicely. Ask questions such as, "Did you really do that?" or, "How did you make that color?" or, "How did you stay within the lines so well?"

The same principle also applies to your older children and teenagers. When they produce a work of which they are especially proud, sit up and take notice. If your son tells you about a great catch he made at the game, ask him about the play instead of saying, "Oh, that's nice, dear."

After one critically acclaimed artistic triumph after another, your kids might be thinking to themselves, "Why limit our exhibits to the kitchen? Work this good should be shared with the entire world—or at least Dad's friends at the office." I oblige, of course, but to a point. I take them to work.

It's a situation reminiscent of those "thoughtful" but crazy gifts you get every year from the in-laws. It might be a lamp, a vase, or a planter in the shape of a fire hydrant. All of these items have one thing in common—they never see the light of day until you spot your in-laws stomping up the walkway. As they ring the door bell, presto, they magically appear out of thin air. But keep a feather duster handy—if they're not dusted, you're busted.

My kids are only mildly interested in my work when they visit the office. What they immediately want to see is their art projects gracing my walls. If you think they're going to forget about those water color seascapes or yarn-covered pencil holders, you're mistaken. That's why I've designated a special drawer in my desk reserved exclusively for my kids' artistic endeavors. When I know my wife is bringing them over for a visit, out they come. They are quickly removed upon their departure—well, not all of them.

HOW DO YOU KNOW
WHEN YOUR CHILD NEEDS QUALITY TIME?
(When his beeper goes off, he needs you.)

One day I was swimming with my son, who was three at the time. Suddenly, my pager went off from underneath a pile of towels on the chair. Before I could pull myself from the pool, my son leaped out, snatched the pager, and hurled it into the pool—the deep end. We could hear a faint gurgling sound as it slowly sank to the bottom. I quickly turned to my son for an explanation. His arms were raised high over his head, palms up, and shoulders back. "All gone," he said.

As I was pondering his fate (perhaps walking the plank—I had plenty of two-by-fours), another beeper began sounding in my head. All at once it came to me—I was getting a bit out of balance myself. I had been putting my career ahead of my kids. My son had made an executive decision—no pager, no interruptions. It was time for a parenting pit stop.

What if God had equipped kids with little pop-up timers? (They work on frozen turkeys, don't they?) As soon as a child needed attention, pop goes the timer. On second thought, God probably knew we'd grow dependent on them. There are no shortcuts when it comes to parenting.

Most children can travel only so far on a full tank of attention. Don't wait until the needle reads empty. Keep "topping off" their tanks. Remember, kids are attention guzzlers. If they have to worry when the next fill up is going to come, they will be continually insecure and needy. Keep their little tanks full, and you'll notice improved mileage figures. The more secure they feel with your love, the longer they can go between attention fill ups, and the more OK they are with themselves.

I'm happy to report that my son no longer flings my pagers when he needs attention—that's what sisters are for. My kids do, however, let me know in a host of other, less destructive but equally effective, nonverbal ways. Here are a few flares your kid might shoot into the air the next time he needs attention:

- Acting up (throwing tantrums)
- Being disrespectful
- Hanging all over you while you're busy
- Hounding you to do something

Just because your child seems to be quietly going about his business, don't automatically assume that he's up to something. He's probably been getting enough quality time and attention from his parents, that's all. Good for you.

FAMILY VACATIONS OR QUALITY TIME FROM HELL?

Are we having fun yet? Despite efforts to block out certain childhood experiences, I unfortunately remember every last detail of our family vacations. The excitement of a great adventure usually lasted about fifty miles, or until the two four-ounce root beer Big Gulps caught up with me.

I felt trapped with no way out. All couped up in a cramped back seat with my grandmother, my brother, Juan (the family terrier), sleeping bags, and an ice chest. And I had to go to the bathroom. "Dad. Paaallleeeaaassseee stop at the nearest rest stop. I gotta go real bad." Understand right up front that getting any dad to stop the car on a family vacation is about as likely as getting a ride in a space shuttle.

Things usually went from worse to miserable. The petty bickering was nonstop and covered everything from where we should eat next to who consumed all of the peanut M&Ms. And that was just my parents. I generally spent the majority of my family camping vacations wishing a huge grizzly would wander into the campground, sniff me out, and carry me off into the woods.

Family outings and vacations are supposed to be fun. As parents, it's our responsibility to see that they remain fun. If that requires an Oscar award-winning performance, so be it. Don't spoil quality time by being a grumpy bear!

5

If You Really Want to Alienate Your Kids . . .
DON'T WORRY ABOUT SETTING BOUNDARIES AND LIMITS

I was pulling into the driveway when I heard "Daddy, watch me!" I looked in my rearview mirror just in time to see my daughter barreling across the street—arms flailing like a wobbly tightrope walker—on her new pair of roller blades. "Nice technique, Tracy. Let's talk."

Here it comes again, she must have been thinking. *Another one of those "You know better than that" talks.* After I explained, again, that she had broken the rules by crossing the street, she looked up at me with with the sincerest of blue eyes and asked, "Why do we need so many rules, Dad?"

"Well, Tracy," I stalled, "for the same reason that sheep need shepherds." For the same reason that sheep need shepherds? Great. Now I was stuck. I had to come up with a good sheep story—

fast. My daughter is a terrific skater but a tough audience. Where's Bill Cosby when you need him?

"Sheep. What sheep? What do sheep have to do with roller blades anyway, Dad?"

At least I had her attention. "Tracy, would you like to hear the story about Mutton, the sheep with the flawless fleece?"

"Sure, Dad," she enthused. "Is this a long story 'cause my friend is coming over pretty soon. . . . What's fleece?"

"Let's go inside, and I'll tell you." She grabbed the largest pillow from the couch, and flopped on it with the grace of a pole vaulter.

Long ago, in a distant land, a sad-eyed, woefully underweight little lamb was born. The ranchers figured he would never amount to much—except perhaps lunch—so they callously named him Mutton.

As time passed, Mutton began to mature. His ragged, sparsely dotted, patchwork coat of wool became thick and luxurious. It wasn't long before the clumsy, ridiculed baby lamb had grown the most beautiful sweater of perfect white fleece in the entire flock.

Mutton was assigned to the finest flock on the vast ranch. Each day their shepherd, Dave, would lead the lambs to the choicest areas for grazing and then make sure they arrived home safely by nightfall. Every member of the flock was instructed never to stray from the grazing grounds. Above all, they were told *never* to go beyond the long, wooden fence that separated the ranch from the great forest—where the fearsome wolves lived.

The rules were clear. The grass was sweet. Life was good, except for the haircuts. Until, that is, the kind old shepherd who had tended the flock for so long decided to retire.

With no qualified candidates to replace him, the rancher published the following classified ad: "Shepherd wanted to tend extremely docile, conforming, and well-adjusted flock. Must have own staff. Dogs optional."

Tom, an unemployed shepherd, read the ad and wasted no time applying at the ranch. His credentials appeared in order, although his last job did seem a stretch—playground supervisor helping teachers round up sixth graders after recess and herd them back to class. But he was hired just the same.

Eager to assert his authority and make a good impression, Tom decided to rent a couple of dogs. "Why wear myself out chasing strays," he reasoned. But instead of going to the local Sheep Depot, which carried a large inventory of tail-wagging, fleece-friendly, sheep herding dogs, he opted on the Junkyard Dog Obedience Institute where he selected two menacing-looking Doberman pinschers. Tom and his Dobies quickly took charge.

One afternoon, after Mutton had been chased back to the flock by one of the dogs, he decided that enough was enough. "What's with this macho attack dog routine anyway?" Mutton complained to a few of his closest friends. "Dave never needed dogs. We always followed the rules. In fact, we're born followers, aren't we? We're not like those mountain climbing goats or grungy cattle—we're sheep."

Mutton began to have rebellious thoughts: *He just keeps us here because it's convenient for him. He wants to stay close to his comfortable little camp and his nice warm tent. It's not faaaiiiirr.* (Even sheep say it.) *The same trees. The same hills. The same sheep.*

Just look at all of that fresh, green grass on the other side of the fence, he thought. *And here we are stuck with those two stupid dogs and Goofy for a shepherd.*

Later that evening, when the shepherd, the flock, and even the dogs were sound asleep, Mutton quietly arose (being careful not to let out an involuntary baaaaa) and tip-toed out for a midnight snack. He chewed mindlessly on the trodden blades as his thoughts drifted to the other side of the fence where the grass was lush and adventure waited.

He cautiously eased up to the fence, poked his head through the rails and took a lingering look around. "I don't see any wolves out there," he whispered to himself. "Tom was probably just trying to scare us with all of those wolf stories. Look at that grass! My, oh my."

If I could only find a hole in the fence or something, Mutton thought, his heart rushing with excitement. With new vigor and purpose he began walking briskly alongside the fence, looking for a weak link and a ticket to the other side.

As he reached the crest of a small hill, he noticed a broken rail. *Maybe, with a running start* . . . Mutton took a deep breath and sprinted toward the fence. With one mighty leap, he cleared the fence and tumbled head over hoof on the other side. I made it! "Baaaaa, baaaaa, baaaaa, baaaaa." He couldn't hold back any more, he was so happy. "Yes, this is the biggest 'baaaa, baaaa' night of my life. Baaaaa!"

Mutton dove triumphantly into the fresh, green blades. "I don't need a shepherd. I have everything I could ever want right here. This is the life. Baaaaa, baaaaa." But after a while his sense of accomplishment was replaced by feelings of fear and guilt. The grass didn't taste as good as he thought it would, there were strange sounds coming from the woods, and what about those wolves?

Mutton decided that maybe this wasn't such a good idea. "I think I'll mosey on back to my side of the fence where it's safe." He was baaaaing uncontrollably now, and, as he turned around, he saw it—a sheep's worst nightmare. A pair of glowing, red eyes peering out from behind a tree. And then he saw the fangs—hungry, white, and dripping with saliva. Wolf!!

As the wolf lunged for an easy meal, Mutton prayed that it would be over quickly. Just then, something inside shouted, "Run, you idiot, run!" And run he did, faster than a sheep had ever run before. The wolf was nipping at his tail like a pair of shears as he reached the fence. With one amazing sheep leap, he sprang up and over the fence. Mutton never looked back; he kept running until he reached the safety of the flock and his shepherd. He was so happy to be home, he even gave the dogs a big kiss.

"What does that story mean to you, Tracy?" I asked, figuring I had spun off a "10" in the children's story telling department.

"That sheep are faster than wolves, Daddy?"

"No, dear," I said, trying to hide my disappointment. "Mutton learned the hard way that rules were there for his own good—his own protection. You know, like not crossing the street on your skates or bike because a car could be coming too fast around the corner. Do you understand, Tracy?"

"Yeah, Dad. I was just kidding. I liked your story. Now can I go play?"

Kids!

THE WHY AND WHAT OF BOUNDARIES FOR OUR KIDS

Tracy finally realized that rules, in the form of boundaries and limits, are there for her own protection. Not unlike the wooden fence that encircled the ranch, boundaries should be designed to protect our children from themselves and from the wolves of this world.

There must also be teeth in the boundaries and limits we set for our kids—certainly not the fangs of a wolf, but consistent and understood consequences for failing to comply with a boundary. Without consequences, all boundaries are destined to fail, and not only kid boundaries, either. For instance, how many of us would "buckle up" if seat belt laws were not being actively enforced?

Limits, rules, and boundaries come in all sizes, shapes, and colors. They can be as sensible as taking along an umbrella on a cloudy day, as rigid as the steel rails of a train track, and sometimes as bendable as your diet when no one is watching. We all need boundaries. Most of us appreciate them. And at times, we all despise them—including our children.

Can you imagine taking your child bowling without first explaining the rules? You give your kid a ball, carefully position his tiny fingers in the holes and tell him "Let 'er rip!"—which he does, only from behind the snack bar. Next, you position him closer to the alley and gently suggest that he aim for those funny looking white things. He sprints down the alley, drops the ball on the pins and shouts, "Strike, right, Mommy? Root beer for everybody!"

If we don't communicate our limits and boundaries, how can we expect our children to make the right decisions? They have no guidelines to follow. No successful models to emulate. No rules. Without boundaries, we've deprived them of the satisfaction of—indeed, much of the motivation for—achieving. Without the proper ingredients for success, they have no idea how they bowled a strike, nor do they care—it's the end result that matters.

Our prisons are bursting with people who were never taught (or refused to learn) boundaries. They have become hardened, with an "end justifies the means" concept of life.

We can either provide our children with a consistent and clear set of appropriate limits and boundaries or mystify their perception of parenting by continually changing the rules. Play fair by making your boundaries flexible when appropriate, realistic, and attainable. If you lay down endless miles of rigid, unrelenting, cold, steel rails, your children may eventually "jump track" and rebel in an attempt to live life with fewer rigid rules.

A BIBLICAL PERSPECTIVE ON BOUNDARIES

Are boundaries and limits biblical? The answer is a resounding yes! The Bible is filled with references to God's boundaries and limits for mankind. For an early example of God's limits, just open your Bible to the book of Genesis. Pretty short Bible back then: "Don't eat the apple!" Easy, right? Well, you know how the story goes. All real limits and boundaries carry consequences or they are merely suggestions.

God's boundaries and limits for our lives were never more apparent, or rigid, than when He said, "Thou shalt not . . ." How much respect would you have for the Ten Commandments if they were called the "Ten Suggestions"? The movie would have starred Don Knotts, not Charlton Heston. Fact is, they could have been called the Ten Absolute Limits and Boundaries—closed to negotiation, interpretation, or mediation. God's firm, but fair, set of boundaries and limits was designed in our best interests.

But God, our parent, can also be flexible in His boundaries. An excellent example of this is also recorded in the book of Genesis: God finally runs out of patience with the wayward people of Sodom. Just as He is about to destroy the city, which has slipped well beyond His boundaries for human behavior, Abraham intervenes on the city's behalf.

Talk about guts, how many of us would have asked God to reconsider at that late juncture? If it were I, I would have said, "OK, God, if you want to destroy the town, it's your call. Give me about ten minutes to throw a few things together, and I'm outta here. You're the boss."

Here's how Abraham handled the crisis:

> Then Abraham approached [God] and said: "Will you sweep away the righteous with the wicked? What if there are fifty righteous people

within the city? Will you really sweep it away and not spare the place for the sake of the fifty righteous people who are in it? Far be it from you to do such a thing—to kill the righteous with the wicked, treating the righteous and the wicked alike. Far be it from you! Will not the Judge of all the earth do right?" (Genesis 18:23–25)

God was probably amused by Abraham's psychological approach, but He appears to appreciate the logic and compassion behind the challenge: "If I find fifty righteous people in the city of Sodom, I will spare the whole place for their sake" (v. 26). Abraham's sense of satisfaction must have been short-lived when he realized how difficult it would be to find fifty righteous people in Sodom. Hoping his luck wouldn't run out, he continued to negotiate with God: "Now that I have been so bold as to speak to the Lord, though I am nothing but dust and ashes [humble approach—nice touch], what if the number of the righteous is five less than fifty? Will you destroy the whole city because of five people?" (vv. 27–28).

God again accepts Abraham's line of reasoning and eventually reduces the number to only ten righteous people. In doing so, God demonstrates flexibility toward His children. Shouldn't we be willing to be flexible parents as well?

How many of us allow our children to negotiate the boundaries we have already put into motion? Assuming that none of us is perfect, shouldn't we be open to the possibility of being wrong—or, at the very least, be willing to give consideration to other points of view? How can we presume to be the "last word" when our Lord, who is perfect, alters His own boundaries under the right set of circumstances?

WHAT FALLS WITHIN *MY* PERSONAL BOUNDARIES?

The following definitions may be helpful in separating our own personal boundaries from those of others. As parents, it is critical to define exactly what is within our own limits and boundaries before we can help our children understand and set boundaries for themselves.

PERSONAL LIMITS AND BOUNDARIES

My feelings	The way I feel, not the way others expect me to feel.

My beliefs	My beliefs, not what others want me to believe
My behaviors	How I choose to behave, not how others would like me to behave
My choices	The choices I make in my life, not the choices others would make for me
My values	My own values, not the values of others
My limits	What are my limits, not the limits that others impose on me
My desires	What I want and expect of myself, not what others want and expect of me
My needs and wishes	I am responsible for my own needs and wishes and not dependent on what others give me.

As parents, it is important that we take full ownership of the majority of boundaries listed above. If we allow our boundaries to be molded and manipulated by others, such as a controlling spouse, our parents, or other strong-willed individuals in our life, we lose sight of ourselves. Without a sense of self, we become human jellyfish who simply drift along with the tide. We become slaves to the needs, wishes, desires, directions, and control of others.

Children are born with certain instincts and needs—and very little else. As they mature, they must rely on us for the rules to their brand new experience called *life*. Perhaps the first boundary was communicating the sense of touch. The first time your one-year-old reached for the candle on his birthday cake, you said, "No, no, hot!" and pulled his hand back. That was a limit imposed to protect your child. Because it was such a sensible limit, he adopted it as his own, but probably not until he got burnt once or twice while your back was turned. He found out you were right.

Let's say, however, that you are a parent whose limits and boundaries can be described as flimsy at best. Everybody takes advantage of you. Your parents still tell you what you should do, what color you should paint your house, and who you should vote for. You rarely voice an opinion and allow your husband to run the household entirely his way—even when you don't agree. People take advantage of your inability to say no. From agreeing to bake three dozen pies for the church charity auction to running the school car pool for seemingly every kid on the block. If boundaries are a problem in your own life, you will find yourself in a weakened "pushover" position when it comes to your own parenting style.

As we saw in Genesis and Exodus, it is a God-given responsibility that all parents introduce limits and boundaries to their children. First, though, we must get a handle on our own limits and boundaries. Only by doing so will we assume enough personal control over our own lives to shepherd our children in the direction of setting their own limits and boundaries.

SYMPTOMS OF KIDS WITH UNDERDEVELOPED BOUNDARIES

Let's take a look at some of the more common types of boundary-starved kids.

The "I Didn't Do It" Child

Children are natural-born blamers and finger pointers. To some extent, most kids will try to dodge blame for something they shouldn't have done. They have no problem with implicating anyone remotely near the scene of the crime. Chronic blaming, however, is a sure sign of an underdeveloped or nonexistent boundary system. Teach your children that, good, bad or ugly, they must take responsibility for their own actions. Let them know that you aren't perfect and that you don't expect perfection from them. This way of thinking should free them up to accept more responsibility.

The "I Better Ask My Mommy" Child

"When a codependent person is dying, someone else's life flashes in front of them." That's an old, if insensitive, line that nonetheless illustrates that codependent people have never really defined themselves. They have adopted the limits and boundaries of others in order to get through life.

Codependency, like a family's good silverware, is usually passed on from one generation to the next. The result, of course, is codependent children who are more comfortable taking on the limits and boundaries of others than setting their own. These kids are often described as "sheep" or "followers" throughout grade school. Later in life they may find it difficult to say no to the pressures of alcohol, drugs, and sex, since they never learned they had a right to use the word *no*.

The "Mopey" Child

Children that grow up without a sense of "self"—as a result of undeveloped boundaries—often exhibit signs of depression. They feel continually "let down" by people because they are entirely dependent on others to meet their emotional needs. As such, they are subject to depression whenever the caretaker is perceived to have let them down. Depression jumps in when their insecurity takes control. They wonder, *Am I still loved?* and, *Who will take care of me now?*

The "If His Head Wasn't Screwed On" Child

Children who are raised without the sense of self—personal boundaries and limits—are often disorganized. But it's a tough symptom to identify, since many children tend to be somewhat disorganized anyway. The warning signs do, however, become easier to spot in older children and teenagers. You may notice a problem in their completing household chores. They may lack the personal discipline to sit at the kitchen table and do their homework. They may have boundary problems in disciplining themselves enough to routinely attend their classes. And they may have absolutely no plans for the future—college or profession.

The "You Bet, I'll Get Right on It" Child

Children and teens who haven't been shown—or given the right—to set personal boundaries and limits often feel resentment. They resent people who exhibit strength, self-confidence, and authority, which is usually you or anyone they perceive as having control. Resentment often manifests itself in these passive-aggressive relationships with parents, teachers, relatives, and bosses.

At the heart of their resentment is repressed anger for not being strong enough to establish their own rights, feelings, limits, and boundaries. They view their will as inferior to the will of others.

Children and teens show passive-aggressive behavior when they announce "I'll do it," despite having no intention of following through.

The parable of the two sons in Matthew 21:28–31 aptly describes this problem. Jesus talks about the father who asked his two sons to help out in the vineyard. The first son says, "I will not," but later changes his mind and goes to work. The second son says, "I will, sir," but fails to show. The second son exhibited a passive-aggressiveness, probably aimed at his father's authority, by telling him he would comply with his request, while having no intention of doing so.

The "I Can't Do Anything Right" Child

And then there's the boundaryless child whose motto is "Why should I risk doing it myself when you'll end up doing it over anyway?" When a demanding, perfectionistic parent presides like a dictator over her children's boundaries and limits, underresponsibility flourishes. Like the child who blames, an underresponsible child reasons that ownership of one's life is impossible, since someone else already has the pink slip. He often lives by the credo, *Why risk it?* In his heart, he knows he can never measure up to his parents' standards, so he might as well kick back and claim helplessness.

These kids are characterized as classic underachievers—you know, the ones whose teachers said something like, "He has a good mind, but he doesn't apply himself." If this sounds like your child, take a hard and fast look into the boundary situation, because a lifetime of underachieving is not a pretty sight. (We'll take a more in-depth look at the pitfalls of not allowing your children to grow up in chapter 8.)

COMMUNICATING LIMITS AND BOUNDARIES

As we have seen, personal boundaries encompass everything we are and all we would like to become: what we like and don't like; what our dreams are about; our prejudice and our tolerance; our joy and sorrow; our passions; our ambivalence. Above all, our boundaries tell the world who we are. Can we wish or encourage any less for our children?

As parents, if we can't make our boundaries and the accompanying consequences understood, how can we expect anyone, much less our children, to honor them? As your parenting partner may have said to you on more than one occasion, "I'm not a mind reader. How am I supposed to know if you don't tell me?" It's our responsibility, as adults, to communicate our needs and wishes that lay within our boundaries. It is only in unhealthy, boundaryless relationships that others take on that responsibility.

There are certain steps, or filters, that parents should follow when establishing rules and boundaries for children. Whether you are just beginning your parenting adventure with an infant or have decided it's about time to begin setting limits with (not for) older children, these steps may be helpful.

Step 1: Model the Limits and Boundaries

Show your children that you respect limits and boundaries—yours, theirs, and others. Practice what you preach!

Step 2: Are Your Boundaries Clear?

Before you can expect compliance to a boundary, be sure your messages are being received. Like a supervisor assigning new responsibilities at work, it is mandatory that you clearly define the new job duties before you can expect your employees to perform them.

Step 3: Are Your Boundaries Fair?

Remember, sometimes we can ask too much of our children. A boundary that isn't fair is a boundary destined to be tested. An example of this is a parent who sets a strict dating policy on a teenager, eliminating any chance of dating until the age of nineteen. Is this a fair boundary? Probably not, by most standards. Is this boundary likely to be tested by the teenager? Undoubtedly.

Step 4: Communicate the Reasons Behind a Boundary

Explain the rationale behind a specific boundary. Your children will be more willing to respect a boundary and your authority when the limit is fully explained. They also tend to be more compliant to the consequences for "blowing" a boundary when they fully grasp the "ground rules."

Step 5: Ask for Compliance

Another example of preventative parenting is to ask your children to do the right thing by observing your limits and boundaries. The time to ask for compliance is *before* consequences are levied for a blown boundary.

Step 6: Is Compliance Possible?

Some parents expect the impossible of their kids. You wouldn't expect two small children, for example, to sit quietly for an hour while you tried on dresses at the department store, would you?

Step 7: Establish the Consequences

Punishment does not necessarily equal consequences, and consequences are not meant to punish. They are intended to teach. For instance, if you choose to go 65 MPH in a 35 MPH zone, you are choosing to break a boundary. If you are pulled over and cited, is that ticket the punishment or a consequence intended to teach you not to speed again? Right, its a consequence.

When you establish consequences, be sure they are consistent with the severity of the broken boundary. For example, it would be extreme to restrict your kid to his room for the weekend for taking an extra cookie after you told him no more. Consequences are supposed to be motivating and fair so that they will have a chance to succeed in their mission—to teach.

Step 8: Explain the Consequences

Don't keep your children in the dark. Let them know up front the significance of an individual boundary. Explain the consequences. It's sort of like when you take out a new certificate of deposit. The banker tells you there will be "a substantial penalty for early withdrawal." Let them know that their willful noncompliance with your boundaries will result in the consequence you discussed. Discussing consequences in advance takes the blame for blowing the boundary away from you and places it squarely on your child's shoulders. After all, he knew what would happen if he chose to break the boundary.

Step 9: Commit to Consistency

In an ever-changing world, consistency is a luxury. Remember how we defined the well-balanced parent as being utterly predictable? This point is never more important than when setting, maintaining, and responding to boundaries. Simply put, What's OK today is OK next month. What's not is not.

THE LETTER OF THE LAW?

As Christian parents, we are responsible for our children's well-being, for keeping them safe and training them up in the way they should go. We're also familiar with Ephesians 6:1–2: "Children, obey your parents. . . . 'Honor your father and mother.'"

Passages such as these can be truly inspirational, but they should be kept in context. Parents often slam head-on into child-rearing problems when they interpret Scripture from a black-and-white and absolute perspective. The Bible often gets put back on the shelf before Mom or Dad reads "Fathers, do not exasperate your children; instead, bring them up in the training and instruction of the Lord" (Ephesians 6:4).

We've already witnessed God's ability to be in complete control while parenting us with a mixture of love and limits. The quickest way to exasperate—indeed, to alienate—our children is to run roughshod over their boundaries or, worse, to completely disregard them. Remember, kids have a right to *I* and *my* words, too.

Boundaries through Control

When a parent employs Gestapo tactics—fear, manipulation, and intimidation—to keep their children sealed away under tight security like a prisoner of war, they may win "the battle of the wills," but, rest assured, they will lose the war. If our children are afraid of us or are afraid of losing our love because they haven't fully complied with *our* barbed-wire boundaries, then fear often gives way to resentment and complete alienation. Don't be surprised when your kid finally tunnels out from under those rigid boundaries, making good his escape from your life.

Parenting with Love and Limits

Love + Limits = security, acceptance, and the ability to be self-reliant. As much as I despise math, this simple but tremendously important equation sums up the essence of well-balanced parenting. If we are forgiving and set reasonable, clear, and consistent limits, our children will develop a sense of security in themselves, their own boundaries, and the boundaries of others. The key is keeping the formula straight. Was that three parts love or four parts limits? Trust me, it isn't as easy as it sounds.

Parenting with All Love and Grace

Parenting with love and grace. It has a certain ring, doesn't it? It sounds like a perfectly civilized approach to parenting—a "Christian" way of doing things. Unfortunately, in the final analysis, it just doesn't work. God knew immediately it wouldn't work for Him, and it won't work for us.

For starters, a child views all grace as a pizza party with quarters-times-infinity for video games and a man in a rat's costume who gives away balloons. And why not? He has passively been given permission to do as he likes without knowledge of consequences for his actions.

Life is good! His pushover parent has allowed him to become self-centered, irresponsible, and disrespectful—what more could a kid ask for? Believe it or not, it is a proven fact that children prefer limits and structure to autonomy and ultimate freedom. Problem is, they don't always realize it.

Parenting with All Rules and Laws

On the other hand (usually the back of a hand), a controlling all limits type of parent has all the sensitivity of a hungry sumo wrestler. We were introduced to this parenting style, along with the pushover parent, in chapter 1—the platoon parent.

Such a parent has enough rules, limits, conditions, clauses, and fine print to wallpaper the Lincoln Memorial. "You want my love? You better earn it, Mister. Get down and give me fifty push-ups! . . . I can't hear youuu!" A kid raised by a platoon parent should seek representation, because it takes a court order to get any grace. These children jump through every hoop imaginable in hopes of earning even a little love and respect. They attempt to do everything right—but mostly to avoid all the consequences of failing.

FLEXING THE DREADED "NO" MUSCLE

Nearly all fathers believe that the first distinguishable words out of their child's mouth were "Da-da." That's OK. Dads are prone to delusions. Remember that nine-inch trout that has swollen to seventeen pounds over the years? Truth is, the word "No" probably sprang from his lips long before "Da-da" or even "Mama."

The reason is simple. *No* was the word he probably heard most often between the ages of one and two. Every time he attempted to insert a foreign object into his mouth—like the family turtle—he heard a resounding "No!" Each time he reached up to yank something off the counter—like the toaster—"No!" If we had used the word "melon" instead of "no," his first words might well have been "honey dew." No, on second thought, a homonym of that phrase ("honey do") will come to mean something entirely different some day—when he's married.

Our children actually possess two very separate and distinct types of noes. They are: (1) disobedient noes and (2) responsible noes.

Disobedient Noes

Disobedient noes are as easy to spot as an elephant in your living room. Unlike many of those gray areas in parenting that leave us mumbling to ourselves in the privacy of our cars, a disobedient no comes gift wrapped in neon colors. It's about as subtle as a really bad pair of your husband's golf pants (like he has tasteful ones).

If you ask your teenager to be home by 8:00 and he counters with "No, I already told the guys I'd hang with them till ten or so," you could file this one under the "disobedient no" file. When you tell your six-year-old no candy before dinner, and you catch him stuffing mega amounts of M&Ms into his mouth, bingo, another disobedient —albeit, nonverbal—no.

Now that you've identified the problem, what's next? A disobedient no should never be ignored or taken lightly. I'm not suggesting that you implement a "Use a *no*, go to jail" policy, but there should be appropriate consequences attached when your parental boundaries have definitely been crossed.

Territorial Noes

A territorial no is a completely different creature. If you own a women's clothing store, for example, you're the owner, the proprietor—it's your territory. You have the right to fill your racks with the apparel you have personally selected. You also have the right to refuse service (or to say no) for appropriate reasons. Children, too, have an inherent right to responsible or territorial noes. Saying no or yes at the right time is an important part of formulating and guarding their boundary systems. When a child's personal boundaries are arbitrarily struck down by the parents, a slough of problems can develop —even at the dinner table.

"No" Boundaries and Vegetables

A friend of mine enjoys relating an incident that involved his five-year-old son and, of all things, broccoli. As he remembers, a large platter of broccoli was being passed around at the dinner table. Everybody took a serving. His son, however, refused his portion as the plate hovered in front of him like an alien vessel.

But Dad was insistent. "You are going to eat your broccoli," he said, placing a large portion of broccoli on his plate.

He again said, "No, I don't want any."

Dad shot back, "No broccoli, no ice cream after dinner" (low blow, cruel and unusual punishment).

With his dad monitoring every bite, he tearfully finished the broccoli. Moments later he would have "the final word" by vomiting it all over the table. This is not an unusual reaction when food becomes the focal point of a broken personal boundary. How else is a child going to lodge a personal protest? Please take notice that I am not talking about a child's refusing to try something because it has a funny color, an odd shape, or he just wanted something else. In this case, he simply disliked the taste.

Empowering Kids with Boundaries

The urge for parents to paint their children into their own personal boundaries is tempting but should be resisted. When you empower your children with a full complement of personal noes, they are free to begin expressing their own boundaries and limits. If your children are forbidden to say no to things that should fall within their proprietary limits, how can we expect them to say no to drugs, to alcohol, to premarital sex, and to other inappropriate behaviors? You will find that when a child's right to his personal no is honored at home, his need to act up with disobedient noes is greatly reduced.

Are There Consequences to a Territorial No?

It may be easier to win the lottery than to achieve a family consensus about dinner out. One child lobbies for hamburgers, while another has mounted a major write-in campaign for pizza. One basic truth remains: They will never agree on the same thing at the same time.

The family arrives at the pizza place (the dog's signature was deemed valid) and orders the "Ultimate Classic Cheese Experience." As Dad is dishing out slices while grumbling about the lack of cheese, the kid who you swear was left here by aliens declares, "No, I don't want to eat here. I want a hamburger."

"That's OK, son. You don't have to eat here," Dad calmly responds. "If you're hungry later, there may be a few pieces left over tonight after we get home." The boy—suddenly remembering what cold, "picked over" pizza looks like in the family refrigerator—reassesses his position and snaps up a hot slice. He found out that there were consequences to his personal no, so he acted in his best interest. In other words, he had a right to say no, "I choose not to eat pizza." But remember one of the laws of boundaries: They usually come factory-equipped with consequences. In this case, the consequence was beginning to look like cold pizza.

The same scenario with a boundaryless parent looks quite different. You can see how the parent's boundaries can determine an entirely different outcome. When the boy says no to the pizza, his pushover mom quickly rushes next door to the burger place and brings back a Big Mac. Big mistake. By giving in to his desire for a hamburger, his mom has ignored and actually encouraged his right to say no. He was stripped of any chance to take responsibility for his actions—to experience the consequences that go along with certain boundaries.

THE THREE C'S OF BOUNDARY SETTING

The boundaries we set for our children should be considerate, consistent, and compassionate.

1 *Considerate.* Parenting is not a dictatorship, so your boundaries should not be arbitrary, unfair, or irrational. Ask yourself, if the tables were turned, how you would feel about the boundaries that have been set.

2 *Consistent.* Your boundary must be the same today as it will be tomorrow. Changing your boundaries for no apparent reason confuses children and could cause them to lose respect for any future boundaries. Boundaries should also be consistent between parents. Mom shouldn't have one set of boundaries, while dad has another. If your children discover these inconsistencies—and they will—you may find them going to the easier parent for a second opinion—or more likely the first and only.

3 *Compassionate.* Children have a need and a human right to know how you arrived at your boundaries. Let them know that you have set the boundaries—especially the unpopular ones—out of your love for them. Be sure they understand (make up your own Mutton story) that boundaries are set to protect, not to make them angry or hurt.

AUTHOR'S NOTE: I would like to acknowledge the many contributions to this chapter inspired by the works of Henry Cloud, Ph.D., John Townsend, Ph.D., and Guy Owen, Th.M., of the Minirth-Meier Clinic West. If you are interested in a more in-depth study of boundaries, I encourage you to obtain the book *Boundaries*, by Henry Cloud and John Townsend (Grand Rapids: Zondervan, 1992).

6

If You Really Want to Alienate Your Kids . . .
DON'T TEACH THE PRINCIPLES OF FAITHFULNESS AND TRUST

We routinely trust our clothes, our cars, our pets, even our kids, with people who routinely fail to uphold their end of the bargain—to properly clean, repair, de-flea, and baby-sit. What choice do we have?

We grouse, we mutter, we gesture in disgust, but to no avail. Finally, we usually just "write them off" as minor disappointments —a part of living. "Good service is hard to find," we concede. So we keep trying and trusting until we find individuals who keep their promises, fulfill their responsibilities, and meet our expectations.

When somebody says, "Trust me," does a red flag automatically deploy in your mind? It does in mine. It's rough finding trustworthy people in today's "me first" world. But the task of trusting can be equally challenging and frustrating under your own roof.

After all, if a hair stylist violates your trust with a really awful cut, you simply let your fingers do the walking. It's more complicated when your child lets you down. You can't just pick up the phone and order a trustworthy kid "to go"—as you would a pizza. "Let's see, make mine extra reliable with a predisposed revulsion to rock concerts and multiple pierced earrings. Oh, and extra honesty, please. Thirty minutes or less? Fine. I'll wait."

You routinely trust

- ✔ The cleaners, who says your jacket will be ready by 4:30, but it's not.
- ✔ The gardener you hire to just "shape" the tree, and you end up with a winter's supply of firewood.
- ✔ The mechanic who says your car is as good as new, and it breaks down four miles from the shop.
- ✔ The hair stylist who says, "Trust me, you're going to love it." And you can't show your face in public for a week.
- ✔ The drive-through "speaker creature" that takes your order. "Two Kids Meals, one hamburger, fries, and an iced tea, please." You leave with four tacos, a shake, and two greasy fries in the bottom of the bag.
- ✔ Your teenager, when he says he's going to the library to study with some friends, and you run into him at the mall.

A trust violated by a loved one, valued friend, spouse, or child packs quite an emotional punch. Disappointment quickly leads to feelings of hurt, anger, and betrayal. That's why it's important that parents be vigilant. Keep the trust you place with your children under surveillance. Make sure it's being handled with care—not spindled, folded, or mutilated behind your back. Don't be blindsided by the chilling realization that your child has a serious problem, or an addiction, that has gone unchecked for months or even years.

When was the last time you inspected the pipeline of trust between you and your children? Was trust flowing freely with minimal supervision and maintenance? Or was the valve stuck wide open, unleashing unwarranted torrents of trust? Was it so clogged and corroded with lies, disappointment, and broken promises that all trust was blocked? Grab your flashlight and don your parenting "hard hat"—we're going in for a closer look.

CONFUSING UNCONDITIONAL
LOVE WITH UNCONDITIONAL TRUST

Parents often lump unconditional love with unconditional trust, but the two are complete strangers. Trusting your kids unconditionally is like giving them a free pass to exceed limits and vault boundaries. Some children will gladly accept a "blank check" of trust, but without any conception of its true value. What was that old saying? "Give a kid an inch, and he'll take your car keys." It's important for parents to settle on structured, yet reasonable, levels of trust, which serve as boundaries against temptation.

For other children who are more insecure by nature, unconditional trust is a heavy burden. They become consumed with the fear of failure; they're afraid they might disappoint their parent.

Whenever I speak about trust, I open with this statement: "Never, ever trust your children unconditionally." When the not-so-muffled gasps from the audience have subsided, hands spring up around the room. "How can you say that?" one parent will ask, while another blurts out, "What kind of a Christian therapist are you?"

Before the crowd turns ugly and mobilizes with tar and feathers, I quickly refer to Scripture: "Now it is required that those who have been given a trust must *prove* trustworthy" (2 Corinthians 4:2).* God is perfectly willing to trust—but not without conditions. He expects tangible proof that His precious gift of trust is being treated with respect. (The audience begins to relax as they begin to trust me.)

Let's face it, if God had trusted us unconditionally, He would never have suspected any wrongdoing in the Garden of Eden. When God asked Adam and Eve why they were hiding, Adam might have replied, "We're just picking daisies, Sir." An accepting, unconditionally trusting Lord might have responded with, "That's nice. I'll create a vase for your flowers."

As a species we're not to be trusted unconditionally. Why do you think God provided so many warnings—and boundaries? Because He knows us. He understands our strengths, but also our

*All italics in Scripture quotations are author's own.

weaknesses. He gave us free will and the ability to make our own decisions, but He also knew we would occasionally mess up and step on the trust of others in the process.

Unconditional trust sounds like a terrific parenting technique, but it just doesn't work. It's like driving through a blinding storm without windshield wipers—all visibility is lost. I'm not saying "Don't trust your children." On the contrary, the goal of well-balanced parents should be to cement relationships based on mutual trust and respect. But do so with both eyes wide open.

EVEN GOOD KIDS MISHANDLE TRUST

If a teenager is constantly treading on limits, busting boundaries, and disregarding the rules, even pushover parents are going to be guarded about the trust they dish out. But what about the kid who does everything right?

Kevin appeared to be just such a teenager. He didn't drink, smoke, or come home late without "checking in." He worked hard at school, made good grades, and associated with a nice group of friends. An active participant in his church youth group, Kevin also enjoyed healthy portions of quality time with his family on frequent outings, including fishing trips and dirt bike excursions. In short, he was a kid you could trust implicitly. Or was he?

What his parents didn't know was that Kevin had used chewing tobacco (known as "dipping") on a daily basis since he was thirteen. Now eighteen, he was finally coming to grips with the severity of his addiction, but the fear of disappointing his parents was nearly as powerful as the addiction.

It wasn't until he traveled to Brazil with a church missionary group that he realized the full extent of his problem. While away he suffered severe physical and emotional symptoms of tobacco withdrawal. He prayed to God for strength in helping to break the addiction and end his feelings of guilt and low self-esteem based in his hidden addiction. However, the first thing he did upon arrival at Los Angeles International Airport was to buy a tin of chewing tobacco from a gift shop and begin dipping again.

"I realized that I couldn't fight the addiction alone," he said. "And I knew it was just a matter of time before my parents learned about my problem from somebody else. I couldn't let that happen."

This realization, more than anything else, prompted his tearful disclosure the next evening at dinner.

Both parents were devastated, but their emotions led in different directions. Kevin's father felt disappointed, angry, and let down. "Unlike my other kids, I had always trusted him completely. I put all of my faith in Kevin. It was hard to believe he could have betrayed that trust."

His mother was less angry than grieved that her son was suffering from an addiction that had dominated his life for years. "A problem he had been trying to solve by himself," she added sadly.

But how could such a close-knit, church-going family be so blind? "He carried dental floss in his school backpack, and in the trunk of his car," his mom said. "There was absolutely no outward sign that he was using chewing tobacco."

His parents immediately took Kevin to the doctor for an examination. While there were early indications of damage, no cancer was present yet. The doctor showed Kevin graphic pictures of the destructive effects "dipping" can have over a relatively short period of time.

"We learned that it's our responsibility as parents to check backpacks, car trunks, and bedrooms on occasion. "Make sure you know what's going on with your children," she said. "You're only fooling yourself if you think the disease of addiction can't strike your child. Don't trust too much."

MOM AND "POP" QUIZ

Based on what we've learned from Kevin's story, how would you deal with the following situation?

For the most part, your sixteen-year-old has proven to be conscientious and trustworthy throughout most of his young life. He has always respected boundaries, including curfews. When something unforeseen comes up, he let's you know with a phone call. He may get teased a little by his friends when he calls home, but he always upholds his portion of trust. And then one night something unusual happens—he comes in after midnight without a prior phone call.

How would you handle the situation? Here are a few options:

A. Let it go. He never had a problem with being late before.
B. Call it to his attention, and then let it be.
C. Discover why he violated your trust and reinforce the boundary.

I'm confident that most of you selected "C." First, let him know that he's still a great kid. Next, convey your concern about his failure to check in. Let him know that you see this as a clear violation of trust and then ask about any uncommunicated factors that may have led to his tardiness. Find out if he even thought about calling home. If he says no, you may want to explore the possibility that he is passively rebelling against your authority, and being late was his way of telling you to back off the control.

Remind him about shouldering his portion of trust and that your trust is directly connected with his faithfulness. Finally, never let a breech of trust with your kids slide. Even if it's only a hairline fracture in the pipeline, your children want—and need—to be held accountable.

TWO STEPS TO TRUST

Real trust between parent and child requires a two-step process. Step one belongs to the parents. Visualize, if you will, *trust* as a door waiting to be opened. As parents, our job is to properly install and hang that door of trust so that it is easily accessible to our children, give them a key, and show them how it works.

Step two is up to our kids. Teach them that responsibility is the key that opens the door to trust. Without responsibility there can be no trust, and without trust responsibility seems pointless. Demonstrate through your parenting style that the more responsibility they demonstrate, the wider the door opens. The door, of course, can slam shut for periods of time while a child rebuilds your trust through his responsible actions.

Trust Builders and Trust Busters

"See ya later, Mom. I'm going over to Ted's to watch the music video awards," Michael says in rapid fire, attempting to escape his mother's response.

"Wait just a minute," she says, just in time to freeze him in his tracks. "Have you finished your algebra homework? Didn't Mrs. Zimmer say that you haven't been completing your assignments on time?"

"Yeah, I finished it on the bus coming home," he covers. "I gotta go or I'll be late. I'll be home around ten."

Once out the door Michael sighs in relief. "I'm sure glad she didn't check my homework."

Sound familiar? Would you have checked the homework before he left the house? Probably, given Michael's history of homework neglect.

Michael's mom was confident she had done the right thing in trusting her son. "I wanted to build trust in him, so I took him at his word."

"Had Michael done anything to build up your trust lately?" I asked.

"Not much," she said, shaking her head. "But if I don't show trust in him, he might end up being untrustworthy."

Her answer exposed a weak link in her parenting style: "If I don't show trust in him . . ." It was clear that she had the trust-building process reversed—a common parenting pitfall. I explained that Michael must *prove faithful* to her trust, not the other way around. "You are trying to make Michael faithful by giving trust he doesn't deserve—or hasn't earned—instead of helping him earn your trust through faithfulness." I think I saw a light bulb going on in her mind.

Tried Any Trust Builders Lately?

If you're looking for an effective way to help your children develop faithfulness to trust, try "trust builders." Trust builders should be kept handy in the top drawer of your parenting tool chest. For example, when your child freely admits to having broken the window while playing catch, you've got yourself a trust builder. Don't miss the opportunity to communicate how much you respect his honesty, and then work with him on his curve ball.

Think of trust builders as bricks. If we use them sparingly— one or two every now and then—we'll never accumulate enough bricks to build anything of significance. Collect enough bricks to finish the project—a living structure of mutual trust with your children.

Oh, yes. Trust builders may be difficult to find at times, but keep looking. They're around someplace. Trust builders are more common than you think. They occur when your kids

- ✓ Do the right thing even though doing the wrong thing would have been more fun.
- ✓ Don't follow the crowd or do something outside your parental boundaries or the boundaries they have set for themselves.
- ✓ Introduce you to their friends.
- ✓ Ask you questions about tough subjects such as premarital sex, drugs, alcohol, or other problems they may be having.
- ✓ Tell you about the "bad stuff"—the things they messed up at school or elsewhere.
- ✓ Talk to you about their troubles and fears.
- ✓ Do what they said they were going to do.
- ✓ Follow the rules.

Trust busters, from a parent's viewpoint, include

- ✓ When you tell them not to ride their bikes in the street, but you see them doing it anyway.
- ✓ When you tell them you don't want them playing with a particular kid on the block, but they do anyway.
- ✓ When you tell them no more cookies, and you find them sneaking some behind your back.
- ✓ When they avoid giving you that deficiency notice from the teacher.
- ✓ When they say they've finished their chores, and they haven't.
- ✓ When they forgot to tell you about the traffic ticket they received.
- ✓ When they break curfew, again and again.
- ✓ When they said they weren't smoking, but you smell cigarette smoke on their clothes. "Oh, I was with a friend who smokes," they explain.
- ✓ When they said they didn't drink at the party, but their breath reeks of alcohol.

BUILDING TRUST, REDUCING DISAPPOINTMENTS

When your child says, "There's something I need to tell you," does a cold chill run up your spine? It does in mine. It could mean anything from a dented fender to an overdrawn checkbook, or worse. What if my seven-year-old found the chain saw again? No parent likes surprises—unless it's straight A's. However, surprise, shock, and disappointment are the common by-products that often accompany unconditional trust and flawed faithfulness.

Hands-on Trust

Again, be sure that the trust you place in your kids is realistic and fully understood. We sometimes assume that our kids are going to be trustworthy without first communicating our wishes and expectations.

The best way to help your children build trust is through a hands-on parenting style. We do this by following up on our kids and by offering insight, encouragement, and direction. A hands-on approach doesn't mean hounding, nagging, or never allowing a child to prove himself trustworthy. It will ultimately convince him that he is, in fact, *un*trustworthy.

Remove Your Parenting Blinders

A teenager announces to his parents that he is going to the mall with some friends. He says he'll be home by 10:00. Since they trust him unconditionally, there is no reason to doubt his word. Their blinders are firmly in place.

Unlike the teenager with the "dipping" problem or the boy with the unfinished homework, the only thing missing in this case were red flares lighting up the sky—there were so many warning signs: he regularly comes home late; he is often sullen, withdrawn, rebellious, and has dramatic mood swings. Still his parents see no cause for concern. After all, he has their unconditional trust. "He would certainly tell us if something were wrong," they reason.

It's not until they receive a late-night call from the police informing them that their son has been arrested for under-age drinking that reality hits home—"My child isn't 100 percent trustworthy?" It's disappointing, sure, but it's reality, not the end of the world. In

Luke 17:1, didn't Jesus warn His disciples that "things that cause people to sin are bound to come"?

Moments of crisis can create real confusion for parents. Some parents will suddenly view their kids as "all bad" after a trust has been broken. Try not to lose perspective, especially when only one or two trust-building bricks have been damaged. There will be many opportunities to repair or replace them later.

After a major crisis of trust, parents often ask, "What do we do now? Set up an around-the-clock surveillance system? Restrict them to their rooms for the next fourteen years?" Seriously, here's their dilemma: They have learned, the hard way, that unconditional trust can lead to serious problems. Sounds complicated, but it's not. The answer lies in becoming a good shepherd of your children.

I once supervised several employees at a counseling center. I trusted each and every one of them, but I soon learned that unconditional trust came with a price tag in lost productivity. I came to realize that when boundaries are not established and maintained, human nature will invariably kick in.

I used to go about my daily routine, checking only infrequently. I wasn't concerned. These were highly trained professional people of sound moral character. I soon learned from another manager, however, that my staff had been going home a little early each night. *What!* I thought, already feeling my face turning red. *How could they do that to me? How could they take advantage of my good nature and easy-going managing style?* Well, it wasn't entirely their fault. I had given them more unconditional trust than they were capable of dealing with responsibly. I had misjudged our basic need for structure. Face the facts: if given the opportunity, many will take advantage of the system in one way or another.

Trust and Moral Character

In contrast, a child reared in a family where trust is based on merit will be far less inclined to violate that trust. When he does, he will experience feelings of guilt because he realizes that he has failed to live up to his end of the bargain. He feels badly for two reasons: he has broken your trust, and he failed to take responsibility for his own actions.

TEACHING RESPONSIBILITY + FAITHFULNESS = TRUST

One Saturday afternoon my wife and I decided we had to do some major shopping—you know, the kind that takes you to a grocery warehouse where, if you want to buy some bagels, you have to buy them in a pack of seventy-two.

Since the kids weren't interested in going, we arranged for a teenager who lived nearby to baby-sit. When we arrived home about two hours later, we were impressed by the attention to detail our kids displayed in destroying the entire house. The kitchen floor was sticky with cherry Jell-o, obviously a new recipe. Plus, every piece of bedding in the entire house had been used to construct a make-shift tent city. And for good measure, there were large clusters of dried macaroni and cheese stuck all over the dog.

A trust had obviously been violated. Did this mean we couldn't entrust our kids to a baby-sitter again? Yes! Seriously, it meant that this was a golden opportunity to reinforce the meaning of responsibility and faithfulness to trust.

Parents will often stop me following a lecture: "I can't trust my teenager any more because I caught him lying. Is it too late to teach him to act in a trustworthy way?" The answer is nearly always no. Remember, almost everybody wants to be trusted. Those who don't suffer from unusual defiant personality disorders (in youth) and anti-social personality disorders (in adults) are capable of being trustworthy. Those with personality disorders have no concern about hurting others, breaking the rules, or participating in criminal activities. For the rest of us, developing trust is a part of our natural makeup. I recommend the following steps for building trust in your kids.

1 *Discuss the principles of trust.* Children are able to cognitively process (understand) the basics of trust by the age of four. Keep it simple. Start letting them see the relationship between trust and faithfulness. The tale of the boy who cried "Wolf!" so often that nobody trusted him is a good story for younger children.

Just because your children are nearing their teenage years, don't assume that your discussions about trust need to end. On the contrary, you may want to redouble your efforts. After all, that's what spring training is all about for baseball players. Even guys with multiyear, million dollar contracts need to review the fundamentals. Keep the underpinning of trust intact and your child's teenage years will be much more manageable.

2 *Communicate your desire to give them more trust.* Let your children know that developing a more trusting and faithful relationship is important to you and them. Help them understand that you are flexible and capable of giving increasing amounts of your trust.

3 *Communicate that increasing your trust is mostly within their control.* Kids and teenagers often think they are powerless to change any facet of their lives. These feelings often stem from early childhood when they were totally dependent on Mom and Dad. As we have seen, some parents actually foster dependency and lack of trustworthiness by failing to give them any trust. They have, in essence, discouraged independence and encouraged them to stay a kid forever. Clue your kids in on the formula for trust: responsibility + faithfulness = trust. Let them know that responsibility and faithfulness fall within their boundaries, while trust falls within a parent's purview.

4 *Communicate the benefits of increasing trust.* There are children and teenagers who shy away from increased responsibility or freedom in their lives. Take the time to point out the benefits and advantages of additional trusts and freedoms.

5 *Ask for their partnership and cooperation in building a trusting relationship.* How many of us forget to ask our kids for their cooperation and compliance? After you've discussed the basic steps of trust with your children, ask them if they have any questions. Ask them if they would like to enjoy more freedom and control over their lives. If they nod their head yes, move on to the next step—catching them doing something right.

6 *Catch them in the act of doing it right.* Remember, trustworthiness doesn't come easily to every child, you may have to break out those trust builders. When they do something worthy of trust, don't pass up the chance to praise them. Older children and teenagers may act embarrassed or pretend like they don't need the accolades. But don't be fooled, they actually love it.

7 *Reward their faithfulness with increased trust.* If you want to train your kids to be unfaithful to your trust, don't acknowledge or reward their faithfulness. On the one hand, you're preaching the importance of being trustworthy. On the other, you're acting as if it's no big deal when they are. This will be seen as an inconsistency in your parenting style, and these mixed messages will confuse and frustrate them. Acknowledging and, more important, demonstrating your appreciation for their faithfulness will lead to greater trust and trustworthiness.

8 *A breach of trust carries consequences.* What is an appropriate consequence for a minor breach of trust? Even though it shouldn't be the wholesale destruction of your trust, it needs to carry consequences. It's really up to each parent to decide. The point is that no consequences will ultimately produce a less trustworthy child.

When you have decided on the penalty for a violation of trust, discuss it with your child. Be positive—there's a bright side. You now have the opportunity to engage in meaningful dialog about something personal. Plus, you can communicate the larger lesson that comes from his deeper understanding of the value of trust. Explain that he can regain your trust with his faithfulness.

9 *Don't lord your trust over your kids.* Remember, children desire and crave trust. And why not? Don't we all want the trust of those we love and respect? So don't be stingy with your trust or make it so difficult to attain that your child gives up on the notion of trust altogether. Like most anything, if trust seems too elusive or unattainable, a child will eventually stop reaching for it.

MOTIVATING FAITHFULNESS?

A colleague of mine came up with a novel method of "hedging his bets" when it came to trusting his two teenage sons. It's not that he didn't have a high level of trust in his boys, but he also remembered how he behaved as a teenager. Scary thought. The method was straightforward, simple, and involved a tidy sum of money. The goal? To keep his boys from drinking, smoking, or engaging in premarital sex before the age of eighteen. Here's how he did it.

When his boys were eleven and twelve, he offered them the following proposition:

1. If you don't smoke before you are eighteen, you will receive $2,000.

2. If you don't drink before you are eighteen, you will receive $2,000.
3. If you don't engage in premarital sex before you are eighteen, you will receive $2,000.

They would receive a total of $6,000 each if they stuck to the rules.

He added, "If you choose to give up the money in any of these areas, I'll understand, but you must be honest and let me know." They both agreed and immediately began figuring out what kind of car they were going to buy with their money—right down to the color.

When the older boy reached sixteen and started going to parties, Dad would get occasional phone calls from his son requesting a ride home. "Everybody around here is smoking and drinking, could you pick me up?" His son was acting in a trustworthy fashion.

One day the younger boy, who had just turned sixteen, announced to his father that he was going to a party and "when the night is over I'm not going to have two thousand dollars." All of his friends would be drinking, he reasoned, and he wanted to try some beer too.

"How much do you suppose a six-pack of beer costs?" his dad calmly asked.

"I don't know, around three bucks."

"How much do you stand to lose if you drink beer tonight, son?"

"Two thousand dollars, Dad," his son said solemnly.

"That's right, son. Do the math and let me know if you really want a two thousand dollar beer tonight. It's really up to you."

At the party, the temptation was strong, but his agreement with his father turned out to be stronger. And believe it or not, both boys went on to collect their reward for being faithful to their father's trust.

It's our job as parents to think about ways to positively motivate our children to be truthful and trustworthy. It might be a special vacation, money, the down payment on a car, or college tuition. Just giving them something to shoot for—a goal—can be the motivating nudge they need.

TRUST DEPENDENCY

Trust breeds independence in your children. Conversely, a lack of trust gives way to a sense of dependence. Remember that door of trust we installed for our kids? As they prove to be more responsible, we can open the door wider to more opportunities and freedoms. This is the beginning of a new relationship within the family. They will still hear the word *no* when necessary, but hopefully not as often. And when they do, there may be discussions or even negotiations on the subject. Discussions and negotiations involve dialog, which is always a good thing between parent and child.

Your child is moving from a "one up–one down" relationship with the parent to a position of increasing independence—a maturing process that will help prepare him for a smoother entry into adolescence and adulthood. With softening boundaries, and an increasing number of structured freedoms, parents should be ready to begin the "letting go" process. As you do, it becomes more important than ever to keep those lines of communication open. Let him know that these new freedoms are earned as a direct result of his trustworthiness. And that as long it continues, he will continue to receive more and more trust.

Parents should begin now to allow their children more room for personal decision making, even in difficult decisions. If your teen makes a poor decision or is unfaithful to your trust, simply tighten up the structure a little. He still needs to know there are consequences when trust is violated.

Sometimes your kids are going to make mistakes that have nothing to do with trustworthiness. For example, I recently purchased a special $150 piece of software I was told my computer printer needed to work properly. I spent three hours installing the software, and guess what? You're right, my printer still wouldn't work. So I called a few more places and discovered that the salesman had sold me the wrong part. I made the mistake, but am I any less trustworthy when it comes to buying software? Maybe a little wiser (very little) but no less trustworthy.

Good luck, and happy trusting.

7

If You Really Want to Alienate Your Kids . . .

FORGET ABOUT DISCIPLINE WHEN THEY MANIPULATE, CONTROL, AND TERRORIZE THE HOUSEHOLD

Parents have grappled with issues of discipline since Cain (mankind's first problem child) flicked his strained peas at Eve. We're inundated by endless theories, deluged with dire warnings, and confused by conflicting advice. If we spare the rod, will we spoil the child? Will a simple swat leave irreparable emotional scars? How much discipline is enough? How much is too much? And on it goes.

Some parents, I suspect, wouldn't mind using the rod on the psychologist who once advised them to spare the child. Seriously, the debate over disciplining our young has raged through the ages. Clay tablets dating back six thousand years describe how the ancient Babylonians handled insolent and disobedient children. According to Dr. Irwin Hyman, professor of psychology at Temple University, their answer was "a swat on the behind."[3]

AGE-APPROPRIATE DISCIPLINE

There comes a moment in every parent's career when baby stops being perfect (in the parent's eyes) and starts being human—capable of making mistakes, even capable of producing parental anger. Someone once said that "babies are angels whose wings grow shorter as their legs grow longer." Do you remember that special moment when your "angel" required a little discipline for the first time?

For one mom, it was when her fourteen-month-old daughter latched onto one of those thick, permanent, red markers. "She began scrawling cute little circles on the kitchen floor that quickly grew to cover walls, miniblinds, lamp shades, and just about every major appliance in the house. Sure, there was anger," she remembers. "It also struck me that I had better develop some disciplinary skills fast, before she wrecked the place!"

Another acquaintance vividly recalled the day his eighteen-month-old son darted outside, turned on the garden hose, and dragged it into the living room, where he proceeded to blast the TV like a fireman at a three-alarm blaze. "Clean, Daddy," was all he said, as Dad's face turned crimson.

Before administering discipline—especially to a younger child—ask yourself the following question: Is my kid really mature enough to comply with my request? Some things are simply out of their realm of compliance.

You wouldn't expect, for example, a child of four to spend hours with you at the mall without growing weary and bored. (I start whining after fifteen minutes.) The message to your child would be a negative one—that you are a parent who expects the impossible.

Unrealistic expectations can generate negative feelings that last a childhood—and don't end there. While on vacation a few years ago, my wife and I stepped into a gift shop filled with expensive looking crystal. As we left the shop my wife pointed at me and started laughing hysterically.

"What's so funny?" I asked.

"You walked through the entire store with your hands stuffed in your pockets, stiff as a statue," she said.

Upon reflection (an occupational hazard), I remembered getting into major trouble as a kid for touching items in gift shops. In fact, I believe the phrase "You break it, you buy it" was coined after a visit to one particular shop full of fragile curios.

My parents might have been better advised to leave Mr. Sticky Fingers home. Most parents know that kids are naturally drawn to knickknacks—especially fragile, glass ones. It's impossible to discipline curiosity out of a kid, so why tempt fate?

Evaluate your child's behavioral characteristics against the "Laws of Boredom, Temptation, and Confinement" (BTC). Before disciplining a child for "acting up," for example, be sure it's not a case of BTC. Believe me, these factors can bring out the very worst in children. Again, avoid placing them in situations that stretch their ability to comply.

TO SPANK OR NOT TO SPANK?
THERE'S REALLY NO QUESTION

Until 1946, psychologists were generally in agreement that discipline, including periodic spankings, was a necessary component for rearing well-adjusted children. Enter Dr. Benjamin Spock (not to be confused with the Mr. Spock of *Star Trek* fame), who confused a generation of parents by preaching permissiveness in his well-meaning work, *The Common Sense Book of Baby and Child Care.*

Finally, in 1976, Dr. Spock recanted somewhat in an article entitled "How Not to Bring Up a Bratty Child." He writes, "The way to get a child to do what must be done is to be clear and definite each time. I'm not recommending the overbearing manner of a drill sergeant that would rub anyone the wrong way. The manner can be and should be friendly. A firm, calm approach makes a child much more likely to cooperate."[4]

I view spanking as just another tool in your parenting tool box. If you were a carpenter, you wouldn't set out to build a piece of fine furniture with only a hammer. Why make the job of parenting more difficult by limiting your resources?

Before we discuss other, more preferable options to spanking, consider the following two questions:

1. What forms of discipline fit my parenting style?
2. What forms of discipline do my spouse and I agree upon?

TOOLS IN YOUR PARENTING TOOL BOX

When was the last time you opened your parenting tool box and took a good look inside? Dig around. You'll find an assortment of useful items that may help you avoid the need for spanking altogether.

Set-Up Avoiders

Parents sometimes tend to "set up" their kids in the difficult (if not impossible) problem of having to abide by unreasonable or unrealistic rules or assumptions. So keep a pair of set-up avoiders handy whenever you're thinking about asking your five-year-old to sit through a seven-course meal without having to go to the restroom every five minutes. Consider the odds of compliance.

Set-up avoiders work well for teenagers too. A friend of mine called saying that he was thoroughly disgusted and upset with his son. "We thought we could trust him," he said, "so we went away for the weekend. Well, Greg, we come to find out he threw a party while we were gone. Worse yet, some of the coins from my collection were stolen."

"Did you tell him he couldn't have a party, Ed?" I asked.

"Well, no. But we shouldn't have to. He should have known better at fifteen."

Again, it pays to ask yourself, "Am I expecting too much?"

Positive Reinforcement/Reward Systems

As we've discussed, catching your child in the act of doing something right is an incredibly effective parenting tool. Parents occasionally complain that they have tried everything in their parenting tool box to no avail. Often, though, they have overlooked the most important tool of all—positive reinforcement. (Stay tuned for more details later in this chapter.)

A Stern Look

For some children, one stern look is all it takes to produce positive behavior. Do you remember some of the "looks" you saw growing up? I always thought Mother had a corner on the "evil eye" market. One look was akin to a near-death experience. Message received—alter my present course of behavior because, if looks could kill, I'm a dead man.

Other children, however, fail to grasp the meaning behind a stern look. They might surmise, *Poor Mommy—indigestion again.* These kids often need a little more stimulus to alter a particular behavior.

Strong Words

The verbalization of disappointment has the same effect on some children as a spanking might have on others. Remember, though, that strong words should never minimize, demoralize, or lower self-esteem. They should be intended to correct a certain behavior right at the scene of the crime. If too much time elapses, you might as well stick your strong words back into your parenting tool box—they're virtually worthless now.

A Stern Warning

Stern warnings can also be effective when other measures have failed. A stern warning tells a child that a simple misdemeanor could become a felony should he continue on his present path. Avoid threatening tones or raising your voice when issuing stern warnings. Work on your best Clint Eastwood impression by remaining calm, cool, and in complete control of the situation. It's his move now— "Go ahead . . . make my day." Stern warnings also give your child a sneak preview of disciplinary attractions coming to a home like his soon.

Time-outs

Let's say your child is bouncing a basketball inside the house. You've tried stern looks, harsh words, and warnings without success. Instead of "blowing up," call a time-out. Send your kid to his room for five, ten, or fifteen minutes. Explain that he should "think over his actions." Don't worry, he won't. Time-outs are really designed to give you a chance to calm down, regroup, and develop your next strategy.

When our kids were younger, we ushered them to their rooms clutching egg timers. The timers served two purposes. First, they could watch the minutes ticking away, which kept their internment from feeling like an eternity. Second, when the bell sounded, look out, they were on the loose again.

Enduring Natural Consequences

"What do I do now?" asked an obviously distressed woman who called my radio show. "My teenaged son won't pick up his room or even bring his laundry down to the basement for me to wash. Then he gets angry because he doesn't have any clean clothes for school."

As you might have guessed, my advice was to allow him to experience the consequences of his actions. "It won't kill him to wear a few wrinkled and soiled shirts," I suggested. "Otherwise, you might still be doing his laundry when he's thirty."

Suspension of Certain Privileges

Before suspending any privilege, do a little brushing up. Make certain the privilege is really something your child can't live without. If you're not sure, ask. Don't be manipulated by a quick-thinking kid who says, "I really miss mowing the lawn, Dad, because it helps me feel close to nature."

If you're determined to slam home a point with laser-like velocity, revoke your kid's TV privileges for the evening. For teenagers, restricting them to the house on a Friday or Saturday night is a reliable way to get their attention. Want to try something on the leading edge of discipline? Make them wear bright and cheerful colors.

Spanking

When all else fails, a spanking may be in order. When I was a kid, my backside sported a seemingly continuous rosy hue. Mom would occasionally get into the act, but it was Dad who usually carried out the sentence. (He popularized the phrase, "This is going to hurt me a lot more than you.")

I can't complain too much, though, because he always granted me a last request. "I want to go to the bathroom!" Once behind closed doors I'd stuff anything and everything—rags, towels, area rugs—into my pants before calmly returning to "face the music."

Come to think about it, my father must have noticed the abnormal bulges protruding from my backside. Perhaps it did hurt him more.

Before you choose to spank, make sure you've run through all the available options in your parenting tool box. Spanking should be used only when you've exhausted all other options.

THE TEN COMMANDMENTS OF DISCIPLINE

1 *Examine the evidence.* When our son was four, he wasn't content with just watching the fish in our aquarium; he preferred a more hands-on approach to the hobby. Unfortunately, this was not always healthy for the fish. I repeatedly admonished him for sticking his hand in the tank, forcing the fish to flee for refuge behind the pump. Suffice to say, I wasn't too surprised the day I found a fish lying flopless on the carpet.

My prime suspect flatly denied any wrongdoing. So slipping into my best detective mode, I began to investigate the "Case of the Flying Fish" as a homicide. My son argued that it must have been the desperate act of a suicidal fish. Under oath he remembered seeing the victim performing dangerous back-flips in the tank. "He must have been showing off for his friends," my son deduced.

Score one for the little "fish grabber." I, too, had noticed my tropical fish leaping out of the water on occasion. The final blow came when my kid pointed out that our tank had no top—"Remember, Dad, you were going to buy one."

With no witnesses, except one tight-lipped dog, my case was in the tank. I tried bright lights, the threat of brussels sprouts for dinner—I even tantalized him with a family pack of M&Ms. He never cracked. The bottom line? Examine all the evidence and interview all witnesses before bringing charges.

2 *Justice should be swift.* Don't make your kids sit on "death row" for hours waiting for a pardon from the governor. I'm not opposed, however, to letting them sit in their rooms and ponder their fate, while I consider the appropriate discipline. Whatever you decide, be sure your discipline is swift.

3 *Don't discipline out of anger.* Try not to discipline in the heat of the moment, when emotions are peaking. In some states report cards actually come with warning statements to parents about reacting out

of anger to a disappointing grade. Before you lose control, call a parenting time-out. Think about it, and seek counsel if necessary.

4 *Keep your word.* Don't make threats you don't intend to keep. If you warn your child that he will be disciplined the next time he breaks a certain household rule, be sure to follow through. You will lose a measure of respect, along with your parental boundaries, by failing to act decisively.

5 *Don't exhume the bodies of the past.* Stay current. Discipline your children for today's "mess up," not the one that occurred last week, last month, or even last year. We've all heard of the "statute of limitations"—a determined length of time authorities have to take legal action against a suspect. If the clock runs out before any charges have been filed, he's off the hook for that particular offense.

Our kids should enjoy the same rights, don't you agree? For example, let's say your teenager was caught shoplifting two years ago. It's not fair to bring up the incident every time he says, "I'm going to the mall." Grace and forgiveness should also enter into your disciplinary style.

6 *Never argue with your kids.* The moment you argue with your children, you've lost. You have empowered them with more authority than they need—or want. Some kids use arguing as a stalling tactic to avoid discipline. They figure if they plead their case vehemently enough, they might get you to reverse your decision.

7 *Punishment should fit the crime.* Don't give your kids the death penalty for a misdemeanor—for instance, if your teenager misses curfew by a few minutes. Any discipline should reflect the severity of the problem. If our son forgets to clean his room, instead of restricting him to his quarters—where he can entertain himself for weeks—we may have him clean his sister's room, too. After he gets through putting away Barbie's entire wardrobe, he usually remembers next time.

8 *Help your kids see their role before you discipline.* Help your kids understand their mistakes and the possible motivation behind the misdeed or misconduct. If an apology is in order, be sure they know why and to whom it should be directed. This ends the case by bringing "closure" to their act.

9 *Don't withhold forgiveness—it becomes manipulative.* Some parents stay mad as a way to remain in a one-up power position over their children. Letting go of your anger and communicating forgiveness helps a child do the right thing next time.

10 *Never discipline your children for an accident.* While out to dinner one night my son was having a particularly bad time with his soda. He had succeeded in spilling it on the table several times. I had no problem with the first time—accidents do happen. But when it happened again, I had to wonder—did he actually *want* to spill his soda? Was it just a ploy to get attention? Never discipline your children over an accident, unless you determine that it was no accident.

LOVE, GRACE, AND BIBLICAL DISCIPLINE

Love and discipline—the two should be an inseparable part of your parenting style. Remove love from the mix and you're left with a virulent, destructive strain of discipline known as punishment.

The Bible is brimming with passages that deal directly with discipline. One theme, however, emerges with symphonic resonance: God has given us a highly sensitive, upper-management-level position. We are to help our children develop an inner desire to do good—a job that ends only after they have matured into adults who live their lives grounded in the values and boundaries set forth in God's word. This requires love, grace, and discipline.

"Discipline your son, for in that there is hope; do not be a willing party to his death" (Proverbs 19:18). We are being instructed, in no uncertain terms, to get going. We are to discipline our children early on, while the clay is still soft and pliable. If we fail in our God-given mission, the result could be the spiritual death of our children.

"Train up a child in the way he should go, even when he is old he will not depart from it" (Proverbs 22:6 NASB). The term *train up* means to dedicate, instruct, and motivate. If we do a good job of training up our children early in their lives, they will be far less likely ever to stray from God's well-marked, righteous path.

FAMILY RULES CONTRACT

Sometimes your best ideas are born out of frustration—or chronic exasperation. Hence the "Cynaumon Family Rules Contract." There we were—four distinct individuals—all with varying viewpoints about how we should behave. I had my ideas, my wife had hers, and the kids, of course, had theirs. Something had to give. It was time to call a parenting time-out.

What about a family contract? Why not spell it out? Let our kids know in black and white just what's expected of them. Let them know the consequences for breaking the contract too. Once agreed upon by all parties, we could all sign and date it.

Huddled around the dining room table like delegates at a peace conference, we began to hammer out the terms of our family contract. We began to jot down all the things that were truly important to all of us. What moral and spiritual issues were at the very core of our family relationship? We eventually brainstormed a list of eleven major areas.

Sure, we could easily have come up with fifty or sixty items. But how many points would our kids have retained? Eleven seemed to be a manageable number for our family. I wasted no time jumping on the computer to create a semiofficial-looking document (suitable for framing) that was signed (with ceremonial Bics) and dated by all parties. The dog served as a witness.

Our family contract now holds a place of prominence on the kitchen wall. It serves as a constant reminder of what constitutes inappropriate behavior. Believe me, it's referred to often. There are times when one child might violate a rule and the other will bring it to his or her attention—not in an accusatory way, but as a matter of fact: "Look, see. You signed it—'I will not swear.'"

Here are the ten commandments contained in the Cynaumon Family Contract. Your list will differ depending on your concerns and the ages of your children.

1. I will not hit.
2. I will not keep secrets.
3. I will not lie.
4. I will not use bad language.
5. I will not use drugs, and, if I know somebody who is using drugs, I'll try to help them.
6. I will treat others with respect.

7. If I make a mess, I'll clean it up.
8. I'll pick up my clothes and keep my room neat.
9. I'll talk to Mom and Dad about my problems.
10. I'll do my homework before I go out to play.

The family contract idea can be amended as your children mature and continue to earn more trust. For instance, you could add a line that says, "I will not drink and drive," or, "I will call my parents for a ride home when others are drinking at a party."

REWARD SYSTEMS

As we've pointed out, positive reinforcement can be a far more powerful motivating force than discipline. It teaches your children that doing the right thing has it's advantages. I call these "reward systems."

Unfortunately, parents often overlook this terrific tool and go straight to a threatening mode—"If you don't, I will . . ."—instead of utilizing a reward system that communicates "If you do, I will . . ."

When speaking to groups about discipline, I usually open with a question: "How many of you have to resort to threats of punishment to get your kids to do their chores?" A few hands shoot up right away, while the rest of the parents look around first to make sure they're not alone. True, it's not always easy to motivate our kids to do their chores. But when was the last time you tried positive reinforcement by rewarding your kid when he does good?

One of my son's chores, for example, is to fold his own laundered clothes. It took a series of gentle reminders over several weeks before the concept finally sank in. One day I discovered that Matt had not only folded his own laundry, but the rest of the load as well. A miracle? No, but close enough. His reward? Praise and ice cream, what else?

Positive reinforcement through a reward system strengthens the effectiveness of your discipline. It balances the consequences of misbehaving with the rewards of doing the right thing. It gives your child a clear choice. You don't have to reward your kid every time he does something good, just the first few times for any new task until you are both sure he's getting the hang of it. The goal, of course, is for your children to do their chores automatically.

An effective positive reinforcement system should contain the following elements:

- ✔ Make sure your expectations are appropriate for her age and abilities. Failing in this area can set her up for failure and frustration.
- ✔ Be sure your child has a clear understanding of your expectations.
- ✔ Let him know that you want to help him do a better job by rewarding him when he takes the initiative or does an exceptional job.
- ✔ Praise her when she does a good job. All too often parents forget how important praise is to a child and how it drastically increases the odds of future successes.
- ✔ Follow through, and don't disappoint.

As usual, the Bible says it best:

> We have all had earthly fathers who disciplined us and we respected them for it. How much more should we submit to the Father of our spirits and live? Our fathers disciplined us for a little while as they thought best; but God disciplines us for our good, that we may share in his holiness. No discipline seems pleasant at the time, but painful. Later on, however, it produces a harvest of righteousness and peace for those who have been trained by it. (Hebrews 12:9–11)

8

If You Really Want to Alienate Your Kids . . .

DON'T WORRY ABOUT BUILDING THEIR SELF-ESTEEM

Mommy, watch me!"
"Mommy, help me!"
"Mommy, I'm bored!"
"There are times when my five-year-old makes me so crazy I could just scream," lamented Dee, whose daughter's need for attention seemed insatiable. "Can't she give me a break? Doesn't she ever worry about alienating *me*?"

Dee, who figured there must be a glitch in her mothering technique, opted for short-term therapy to help her quell her daughter's "unreasonable" neediness. "I've always given her lots of attention," she told me during our first session. "Why has she suddenly become so relentless in her demands of my time?"

She complained that her daughter rarely allows her a moment's rest. "I can't even pick up a magazine without being interrupted by a silly request or a demand that I look at her very latest crayon creation."

But how did she respond when her daughter was especially proud of something—such as a special crayon drawing? "I usually say 'That's nice.' Or if I'm really busy I might ask her to 'Show Mommy later.'" Dee admitted that she was careful never to give her daughter too much encouragement, "or I'd never get any peace."

She believed, as do many parents, that the more attention a child receives, the more they want. Just the opposite is true. The "don't give too much, because they'll just want more" approach communicates a tremendously alienating message.

When a parent perceives her child's need for attention as intrusive or demanding, the first step is to explore the parent's own neediness. I have found that these situations are often linked to the parent's own sense of unmet needs dating back to his or her own childhood.

Sure enough, Dee recalled that many of her childhood needs and requirements for attention routinely went unanswered. Her parents might as well have said, "Go away, kid, you bother me," or, "Not now, I don't have time."

She finally recognized that she was allowing her unhappy childhood to adversely influence her own parenting style. This awareness put her in a far better position to "catch herself" before she slipped into her former negative and minimizing ways.

CANTEENS, FLOWERS, AND SELF-ESTEEM

What do canteens and flowers have to do with self-esteem? If you're an adventuresome child of five, plenty.

The morning was brisk, sunny, and anxious to embrace a freckle-faced boy named Benjamin, who had just trooped into the kitchen with his semiofficial, slightly dented, Cub Scout canteen. "Can you fill it up, please, Mom?" he asked, while peeking through the miniblinds at the kids who were staging next door for the big adventure. "We're going up the hill in back of our house to pick wild flowers and look for pretty rocks for our moms—you, too, Mom," he beamed. "I'm going to need my canteen 'cause I'm going to get real hot picking flowers and finding rocks."

His mom, who was busy preparing a shopping list, stopped and somewhat disgustedly took the canteen from his outstretched hands. She stuck the canteen under the faucet and, instead of topping it off, filled it up only halfway. *A five-year-old should be able to fill his own canteen from the garden hose,* she thought.

With compass in hand, a bag for his rocks, and a partially filled canteen, Benjamin joined the others who had created a base camp under the old tree swing behind his house. Before mounting their assault on the short hill, the climbing party decided to scour the lowlands for flowers. Benjamin soon grew thirsty, and proceeded to chug from his canteen until it was bone dry. *Yipes,* he thought, *I better hurry home and get some more water or I might die of thirst.*

He sprinted back to the house, pushed open the screen door, and darted inside before it slammed shut again. "Mom, hurry, look what I picked for you, and I need some more water," he said, trying to catch his breath. *He's back already?* Mom thought, shaking her head. *I was looking forward to a little peace and quiet.*

"These are for you, Mom, and fill 'er up, please." His mom looked at the weeds in one hand, and the empty canteen in the other, and said, "That's nice, dear, but how many times have I told you not to track your dirty footprints on my kitchen floor?" She finally took the ragged bouquet without a word. She was afraid that if she made too big a deal of them he would be bringing home all manner of plant life and expect her to stick them in vases.

His mom took the canteen and hurriedly filled it, but only halfway again. Twisting the cap on tightly, she sent him on his way telling him, "Get your water out of the garden hose next time, OK?"

Thirty minutes later he was back at the screen door. "Hey, Mom, I'm out of water again, and check out this neat lizard I caught."

For children, self-esteem is like water in a canteen. The more water you put in the canteen, the longer your child can go between fill ups. The same can be said about attention. If you ration the attention you give your kids—never giving them quite enough—they will constantly be coming back for more. They will have difficulty getting any farther than your own backyard before their canteen of attention is empty again.

Don't worry. An accidental overdose of love, acknowledgment, and praise won't harm your children. Go ahead, make their day. "That's a *great* drawing! I can't believe you did it by yourself. Can I take this one to work? Wait, sign it for me first, OK?"

Feel free to "top off" their canteens with the encouragement and attention necessary to build healthy self-esteem. Sure, it takes a little longer, but they'll travel much farther between fill ups.

A Snapshot of Self-Esteem

Most of us have used those "quickie" one-hour photo shops on occasion. Just drop off your film and an hour later, double prints of your son making rabbit ears above his sister's head—on glossy paper no less. In a psychological sense, self-esteem is similar to a photographic process—one that begins just after birth and takes years to develop.

You've probably seen those time-lapse exposures of the moon. The camera is placed on a tripod, the picture is snapped, and the shutter remains wide open throughout the evening. The photograph reveals the moon's predictable path across the night sky.

The time-lapse image of a child's self-esteem is far less predictable. An underexposed print could result in a child with a poor sense of self, or low self-esteem. In contrast, an overexposed negative might produce a grandiose or narcissistic "ego monster."

As parents, all we can do is to be sure that our focus is clear and that the subject—our kids—is always in the viewfinder. The goal, of course, is children who grow up with properly exposed self-esteems.

What exactly is self-esteem? For children and adults (who else is there?), self-esteem is a barometer of self-worth. It measures the way we view ourselves and others. If your life were a movie and you were the critic, how would you rate the importance of your life story? Two thumbs up for significance, capability, and worthiness or a definite "Don't see" for indecision, self-doubt, and a poor attitude? Work on the script. Go back to editing while there is still time.

Moms Get the Self-Esteem
Ball Rolling or Stop It in Its Tracks

Listen up, Mom. You get to take the first picture of your baby's emerging self-esteem. Make sure there's film in the camera, and, in my wife's case, make sure the lens cap is removed.

There's no doubting a mother's influence—both verbally and nonverbally—on a newborn's self-esteem. If she responds to her child's needs in a reassuring and relaxed way, the baby will associate this calm and confident style with his own sense of security. Mom has proved that all is well in the world. However, if Mom gets nervous, insecure, and anxious each time her baby cries, or delays in picking him up, both parties could be in for a long childhood. The mother may feel inadequate, but the long-term implications for the baby are even more serious—such as stunted self-esteem.

Remember, a baby doesn't begin to individualize—become its own person—until about the five- or six-month mark. Until then, he remains physically and emotionally linked to his mother. Gradually, though, he begins to notice a difference. *Ummmm, maybe I'm not the same person as Mom,* he ponders. *We don't look that much alike, and she eats lots more interesting stuff than these jars of mashed-up veggies.*

You might notice your child arching his back, straining to get a better look at you while being held. "OK, you're Mom. But who on earth is that person behind you? Please tell me that's not Dad. He's the one who picked out the Great Moments in the Super Bowl wallpaper, isn't he?"

The Wonder Years

The first five years of life are perhaps the most critical in terms of your child's emerging self-esteem. While you are building a trusting relationship with your child, he is widening his horizons—going places, meeting people, making friends, doing lunch.

Your child begins to interact with siblings, family members, people at the day care center, preschool teachers, baby sitters, even the guy next door who is constantly borrowing your tools. They all influence (to varying degrees) the way your child views himself, the world, and his role in the family.

SELF-ESTEEM BUILDERS

Let's dust off a few very useful parenting power tools that I call "self-esteem builders." Be sure to keep them in a convenient place in your parenting toolbox.

Primary Self-Esteem Builders:
Ages Zero to Two (Preverbal)

Physical closeness

The simple process of holding, cuddling, and touching a child from birth to the age where they get too big to pick up and would rather eat strained peas than be cuddled provides a sense of self-esteem, security, and love.

Affection

Hugging, kissing, and playing—you name it. Parents often show affection to infants in a variety of positive ways. These are constant, effective, and essential reminders of your love and approval.

Talking

As we discussed in the chapter on communication, talking to your children is a tremendous way of nurturing their budding self-esteem. This also applies to kids who are too young to ask for a quarter for the video games—you know, six months.

Smiling

When a parent smiles and laughs with an infant, the child often does the very same things in return. Smiling is a powerful reminder of a child's goodness and your approval. Plus, what a power trip for Junior! He is able to make Mom and Dad contort their faces simply by acting coy and being funny. Of course, face contortions are common around changing time as well, he notes.

Laughing

A laughing baby is a happy baby, or one who knows that Dad has to change him soon. A commonly shared trait by children and teenagers suffering from poor self-esteem is a repressed sense of humor. We call this a "dulled affect." They are unable to laugh at themselves or comical situations because humor forces them to "open up" to the world.

Some children, however, use humor as a defense mechanism to keep people at a distance. The stereotypical jolly, overweight kid may be a "cut up" to others, but his jovial exterior may be masking sadness and a self-esteem that is bordering on disastrous.

Secondary Self-Esteem Builders: Ages Three to Five (Postverbal)

Physical Closeness

No changes here. Children are no less dependent than infants for positive reinforcement from parents who are physically close.

Affection

Don't back off on the hugging, kissing, and playing just because your child is no longer a cute, cuddly, little baby.

Praise and Affirmation

Positive affirmation begins to play an increasingly major role. Children actively practice their approval-seeking methods and look to you for affirmation of their real value. Remember, young children have a high minimum daily requirement for positive strokes.

Structure = Rules and Limits

Whereas children crave boundaries during these years, they do their best to test those limits. As we've discussed in previous chapters, consistent structure heightens a child's feeling of well-being and security.

Correction

Just setting boundaries and limits isn't enough—a child needs to understand the value, rewards, and consequences of following, or not following, the rules. If correction and discipline are properly balanced, a child realizes a greater degree of self-esteem through compliance and conformity with the established rules.

Smothering

We'll take a closer look at overprotecting (smothering) children in the next chapter. For now, remember that if we don't trust our kids enough to allow them to experience new things, which means risk taking, how can we expect them to develop healthy self-esteem? Remember, the two main elements of self-esteem are self-confidence and self-image.

Modeling

Modeling simply means "setting an example." Parents who have a healthy (not overinflated or undervalued) sense of themselves will naturally pass along that self-esteem to their children.

Time

Perhaps the most effective self-esteem builder in your parenting tool box is the use of quality time. Spending time—sharing a closeness with your children—emits a ringing message of significance, importance, acceptance, and love.

Ongoing Self-Esteem Builders:
Ages Six and Up (Wish they weren't so verbal)

All of the self-esteem builders outlined in the postverbal section also apply to children and teens six and older. The challenge for parents is that most older children and teens are reluctant to admit that they still crave attention—but we know different. Here are a few additional self-esteem builders that should be squeezed into your growing parenting tool box.

Increasing Accountability

A child's self-esteem is directly proportional to the amount of faith and trust a parent provides. When a parent validates that trust, self-esteem flourishes. If trust is withheld, for whatever reason, self-esteem "takes it on the chin."

Remember, one of the favorite expressions a teenager uses to try to gain increasing accountability is "You don't trust me." This phrase should be met with enthusiasm because it presents an opportunity for your child or teen to prove to you that he can handle increased accountability.

Self-Image

Children in the secondary phase of development (ages two through five) need to know that they are cute, smart, good, and so on. Don't worry, they'll take your word for it.

It's a different story with older children and teenagers. They compare themselves to everyone. They begin to notice physical imperfections. They become gangly, awkward, or pudgy. Once baby-smooth skin now requires an arsenal of ointments. There's more. Puberty marks the onset of facial and body hair. Sexual development brings about irrational emotions. And finally, a cracking voice, pimples, and raging hormones can put self-esteem "on the ropes."

When too many unanswered blows have landed squarely on your child's self-esteem, punch back! Whip out those self-esteem builders and shower your kid with all the "atta boy's" you've got.

Reduce the Negative

Discover the "esteem busters" in your child's life. It may be a weight problem for one child or a lack of coordination for another. Then, as the song goes, "accentuate the positive and eliminate the negative." For every esteem buster find at least two esteem builders. Help them find what they do well, and encourage them to stay with it.

Dads, Don't Pull Back

As we've discussed, dads tend to withdraw from their daughters as they enter adolescence. The timing couldn't be worse. Your preteen or teenager needs the physical and emotional closeness of her dad more than ever. "Pulling back" can erode an already fragile self-esteem. She may feel, on some level, that she's not Daddy's cute little girl anymore. She feels unloved.

AN ACCURATE SELF-IMAGE, FALSE PRAISE, AND EGO MONSTERS

Parents need to be sure their children understand the boundaries, limits, and rules they've established. Consistent limits provide kids with the yardstick they need to measure and evaluate their own performance. Every success builds a little more self-esteem. Every failure, if dealt with honestly, helps them identify and ultimately correct their mistakes. Praise for praise's sake can lead to grandiosity and a loss of direction.

Mr. and Mrs. Hopper and their son, Tony, entered counseling to help their teenager deal with his bouts of depression that resulted from having been cut from the school's soccer team. Tony was acting up in the form of "ditching" school, cursing, temper outbursts, and slamming doors. First, I spoke with Tony alone, while Mr. and Mrs. Hopper waited in my outside office.

"So, Tony, I understand you're having a tough time these days. Your parents think it has something to do with soccer. Is that true?"

"Yeah, it's true," he said. "I've been playing soccer since I was six, and this is the first time I've ever been cut. It's that crummy coach. Ever since I told him he should be playing three forwards instead of two, he's wanted me off the team. He's doesn't know how to coach."

Next, the parents. "Is Tony a good soccer player?" I asked.

"Well, he's not great, but he's not bad either," said Mr. Hopper.

"Let's be honest, Jim," interrupted Mrs. Hopper. "Tony isn't really a gifted athlete. Most of the boys I saw at tryouts seemed to be better. In fact, I tried to get Tony interested in going out for another sport."

I asked the parents if Tony had shown more ability in previous years. "No, he's always been just average," replied Mrs. Hopper.

"Was Tony aware that he was only average?" I asked.

"No way," said Mr. Hopper. "We always made him feel like the star. You know, for his self-esteem and all. Wasn't that the right thing to do?"

The Hoppers learned the hard way that it's one thing to make your children feel important and another to convey an inaccurate sense of themselves. When the high school soccer coach delivered the first "reality check" to Tony by cutting him from the team, he was unable to accept the truth. His parents had inadvertently created a grandiose little "ego monster" with a vastly distorted sense of self-worth.

If you're a parent who celebrates each time your kid does something—even if it's just OK—by "striking up the band" and throwing a party, the actual value of that accomplishment may be greatly diminished. Worse yet, your child could be in for a destructive "free fall" when he discovers the truth.

Don't fool yourself—children know when they do something spectacular. They also have a good idea when they do something just fair. How? By evaluating themselves in relation to their peers. If a parent continually exaggerates a child's accomplishments, and the child realizes he's only average, confusion results.

Some parents believe that continually "pumping up" their child by referring to him as being "cute" or "smart" is enough to build a positive self-esteem. Eventually, however, he will look to others for a more balanced perspective. He instinctively learns that he can't get an honest appraisal from Mom or Dad. By all means, praise your children when they do good, but balance that praise with honesty and correction when they've erred.

An accurate self-image allows a child to feel positive about the things he does well and unsatisfied in the areas he's weak. If he believes that everything he does is awesome, why should he seek to improve?

God repeatedly communicates the importance of not deceiving ourselves. "If we claim to be without sin, we deceive ourselves and the truth is not in us," (1 John 1:8). When children are secure in their parents' unconditional love, they are free to make accurate self-appraisals. This helps to foster and build healthy self-esteem. They feel good about their strong points and are free to work on their weak areas without fear that love and relationship may be withheld.

LABELING

A child's self-esteem can be adversely affected by the negative cues they receive from others. Many children between the ages of two and five view themselves and others as either being all good or all bad. This concrete way of thinking doesn't allow for just "writing off" an insensitive or negative comment. Indeed, an off-handed comment from a callous teacher, coach, parent, or another child could create feelings of inferiority and low self-esteem that last a lifetime.

A couple once asked me to help them make a difficult decision about their child's schooling. They were trying to determine whether they should remove their six-year-old son from his regular class and place him in a special, remedial program for academically slower students. A series of tests indicated that the child was bright, alert, and well-adjusted. There were no physiological problems, such as hearing loss, poor eye sight, motor uncoordination, or learning disabilities. The only real evidence was his school work—it was either sloppy or riddled with mistakes.

We were essentially left with two options: place him in a special program where the kids were working at his level or below, or help him discover why he gets so far behind and is then forced to rush through his work. His parents listened intently as I discussed the potential stigma, or blow to his self-esteem, attached to being separated from his class and classmates. Would he feel inadequate because he wasn't as bright as the others? Or would his self-esteem actually rise in a setting with less pressure?

But before a final decision was made, I recommended that they get some private tutoring in his weak areas—such as math. In the meantime, we had to learn why he was falling behind. Was it daydreaming, poor concentration, or something else? While we were still looking at the possibilities, he was responding extremely well to the tutoring. He was able to remain in his regular class and his work returned to an acceptable level.

The most severe damage caused by labeling often occurs at home. An off-handed remark from a parent, such as "You're not as smart as your sister" or "You'll never amount to anything," can lead to major problems associated with low self-esteem. Negative labeling usually begins with some form of minimization that plays over and over in a child's mind. This negative tape recording continues to play until it has been erased by the parent or by outside intervention. Some children discover for themselves that the message was wrong, but often only after years of insecurity and low self-esteem. The sad truth is that many parents are completely unaware of their labeling and potentially degrading parenting style.

NEGATIVE TRANSFERENCE

Negative transference is another esteem buster in kids. As with so many other things, kids learn by example. If a parent has a poor self-image and is constantly complaining about the job, his weight, or other personal problems, a child may adopt that same negative attitude.

Let's say that one or both parents are constantly talking about their weight problem. Even if the child has an ideal weight, he may actually begin to feel fat and secretly start dieting. Try to work out your problems with self-esteem before your kids try them on for size.

SIGNS AND SYMPTOMS

Symptoms of Healthy Self-Esteem

Not Easily Driven to Tears

Certain stages of childhood, especially preteen and early teen years, can become an emotional rain forest. Tears are common during these years. If your child has healthy self-esteem, however, she will be less emotionally impacted by negative comments, failures, and disappointments.

More Than One Friend and Often Multiple Friends

Children with healthy self-esteems are generally able to make and maintain friendships. They are also more inclined to play with more than one friend at a time rather than trying to isolate with and monopolize a single friend.

Does Well in Social Settings

Young children with good self-esteem are easy to spot. They walk into a crowded playroom and begin playing with other kids right away. Older children and teens will more naturally gravitate toward social events, such as dances, group activities, and youth groups at church.

Risk Takers and Explorers

Kids and teenagers with healthy self-esteem are able to take risks and face failure because their self-image doesn't hang in the balance.

"Up-beat" Personality

Kids and teenagers with healthy self-esteem have a positive frame of mind most of the time. They never have to ride that emotional roller coaster, because they are less dependent on the opinions and acceptance of others to make them feel good.

Signs of Low Self-Esteem

Overly Concerned with Perceived Physical Problems

Kids and teenagers with poor self-esteem tend to fixate or obsess about their physical self-image. They complain about their ears or nose, and may even want to have something surgically corrected. They frequently don't understand how anyone could possibly like them, much less want to go out with them, the way *they* look.

Prefers to Spend Time Alone

Being alone is safer for a child or teen who has low self-esteem. The last thing in the world they want to be is social. Socializing would mean taking risks and becoming more vulnerable, which could lead to being hurt. Thanks, but no thanks.

Shyness

There's a difference between shyness and an overpowering need to spend time alone. The shy child is under constant emotional discomfort while in the company of others. They are preoccupied with the fear that their inadequacies will be discovered, which inhibits their ability to socialize.

These kids will do anything to keep from looking you in the eye when conversing. They'll look at the ground, kick at the floor, twist an article of clothing, and fuss with their hair. They avoid eye contact at all costs, as they believe it will allow others to see their numerous faults. It simply creates too much anxiety.

Non—Risk Takers

It's useful to remember that risk equates to pain in children and teenagers with low self-esteem. Their motto is, "If I can avoid it, I can stay safe," or, "No pain . . . no pain."

Choice of Friends Leaves Something to be Desired

Has your teenager's taste in friends suddenly changed? Are his new friends too disgusting to be in a rock band? A teenager who abandons an appropriate set of friends for an inappropriate set of friends (whatever your standard for inappropriateness) is speaking volumes about his self-esteem. For example, he may feel safer and perhaps more adequate in this new, somewhat lower-class, group of friends.

Avoids Conflicts

For children with low self-esteem any conflict or disagreement quickly escalates into a painful experience. They generally react emotionally, and guard their real feelings and opinions like a soldier guards a fort. They take everything personally.

Codependency

Who qualifies as a codependent child? Any nonrisk-taking, non-assertive, boundaryless, insecure little person (teen or adult too) who is more interested in pleasing his parents than in being happy.

Unfinished Projects

Children and teens who never finish projects, chores, school work, and other commitments are often afraid of failure. This flip side of the insecurity coin is that they may also be afraid of succeeding. Either way, avoiding accountability makes a child with low self-esteem feel safer.

THE SELF-ESTEEM/DEPRESSION CYCLE

As a police officer, nothing was more emotionally wrenching than investigating a teen suicide. In every case, low self-esteem was the leading player in the tragedy. In the book *Adolescent Suicide: Assessment and Intervention,* coauthors Burman and Jobes discuss the predominant link between poor self-esteem and teen suicide. According to the authors, other elements also weigh heavily in a teenager's decision to attempt or commit suicide. Some of these supporting traits include poor parental relationships, substance abuse, shyness, codependency, and broken or unrequited love.[5]

Why should parents need this information? Some parents attribute their child's low self-esteem as "just a phase" or "hormones acting up." I pray I never hear another parent say, "If only I had paid more attention, he'd be alive today."

SPIRITUAL GIFTS AND SELF-ESTEEM

Discover where your children's spiritual gifts lie, and steer them in that direction. In the process, be mindful not to live out your unfulfilled fantasies through them—such as becoming a great ball player, evangelist, or possibly even the church pianist.

Karen

Karen dreamed that her daughter, Jenny, would one day become the pianist at church. When she was five, she was enrolled in private piano lessons. The little girl studied hard, often foregoing play to practice daily. Friends and family were surprised and impressed with her ability to learn and play complex classical pieces. Her mom was proud. Her dream was on course.

The years went by, and Jenny continued to labor countless hours a week at the piano. She was sixteen when her mom gave her the big news—she had been selected to be the new church pianist. Instead of joy, Jenny's heart sank. She knew she could read music all right, but she simply didn't have the talent to "play by ear"—a necessity at her church, since the music director often improvised, requesting a song that wasn't on the list for the day.

She was terrified, but she also knew how important it was to her mom. Finally, that fateful Sunday came. The pews were full, and Jenny's mind was spinning. Her right leg, the one that worked the sustain pedal, was shaking uncontrollably. *What in the world am I doing up here?* she thought. The choir began to sing, and she began to play. She was doing it! Everything was going fine, until the director decided to lead the congregation in a song she hadn't practiced. "I just sat there, and let the organist take over. I simply didn't have the ability to 'wing it.'"

Despite the embarrassment, she tried to memorize as many church songs as possible. Invariably, however, at least one unknown song would be added at the last minute. It was hopeless. Finally, after three excruciatingly long months, the director politely informed her that maybe it would be best to step down. "Thank goodness!"

Although Jenny had done her best, she simply didn't have the natural ability to "play by ear." To this day she refuses to touch a piano. And she would never have one in her own house.

Kelly Ann

On the other end of the esteem spectrum are children whose obvious God-given talents are allowed to go unexplored, even after they have been discovered. Kelly Ann was such a fifteen-year-old.

An artful composition of spindly arms, flailing elbows, and skinny legs hinged by knobby knees—Kelly Ann wasn't exactly a natural born athlete, a fact that never detoured her from participating in sports, however. Softball, basketball, track—she loved them all. And she often pushed herself well beyond her limits trying to improve. But all the desire in the world couldn't help her throw a baseball, sink a basket, or, at times, even run in a straight line.

Sadly, her competitive spirit was never enough to overcome an almost comedic lack of coordination. She was forever tripping, stumbling, falling, and otherwise becoming tangled in her own feet. When playing softball, the opposing team would scream, "Hit the ball to Kelly! She'll never catch it!" She usually obliged. And, of course, she was perennially passed over when teams were selected. Sometimes the two opposing captains would flip a coin to see who would be "stuck" with Kelly Ann. Even her parents told her to forget about sports and concentrate on school, though she was already an A-student in her freshman year.

Despite the knocks, "put downs," and lack of support from her parents, Kelly Ann continued to pursue athletics for the sheer joy of competing, although it was usually against herself. She remained optimistic that one day she would find a sport that suited her. "Perhaps swimming," she pondered.

When swimming became an elective class in her sophomore year, she wasted no time signing up. "I'll do better in the water," she told herself. Eager to learn, she soon mastered the basic swimming strokes. Her technique, her kick, her breathing were flawless, but she was painfully slow. Unable to generate any speed through the water, she continually finished last in every race and every event. Disappointment was finally taking its toll on the teenager. She was starting to think her parents were right all along about sports: "Maybe I *have* been wasting my time."

The last swimming class of the semester fell on an especially grey Tuesday morning in October. As usual, Kelly Ann was the first one at poolside. She had always made it a point to take a few practice laps before class, anything for an edge. As she walked to the pool, towel draped over her shoulders to fend off the chill, she looked up at the diving platform that stood high above the swimming facility.

"I wonder what it would be like . . ." Before she knew it, she found herself making the spiraling thirty-foot climb to the top of the platform. "At first I was terrified. The pool looked no bigger than a small pond. The heated water was shrouded by a thin layer of mist. It really looked beautiful from up there. Somehow, I wasn't scared any more." Without thinking twice she walked purposely to the end of the platform, paused, took a deep breath, and pushed off. Kelly Ann's springy legs—so ineffective in other sports—propelled her well beyond the platform, and high into the air before aiming downward for a perfectly perpendicular descent to the surface. Her slight frame, like an arrow piercing the water, created scarcely a ripple.

She was exhilarated. "I did it!" she exclaimed. "I really did it!"

By now a coach had wandered out to the pool just in time to witness Kelly's private dive. "How long have you been diving?" he asked.

"Ummm, well, just today, I guess—and a few times at friends' houses," she answered, shivering not from the cold, but from the excitement of her achievement.

"Have you ever considered going out for the diving team? I think you have the potential and physique to be a fine diver. Interested?"

She was ecstatic. Finally, a sport where her body didn't betray her. A sport where she was actually wanted by others. It was too good to be true. She was so anxious to tell her parents that she knowingly missed the bus and caught a ride home with a friend.

She burst inside the house bubbling with enthusiasm over her unlikely triumphant. "Guess what happened today at school!" she gushed, not waiting for a response. "The diving coach wants me to try out for the team! Isn't that great?"

Her father's normally round eyes became slits as he looked down, slowly shaking his head disapprovingly. "We've tried to be patient with your little hobbies, Kelly Ann, but we draw the line at diving," he said sternly. "There are more important things in life, such as studying! There will be practices and diving meets. We don't have the time to shuttle you all over town—and neither do you!"

The next day, she thanked the coach, respectfully declining his offer to try out for the team. "My parents don't think it would be a very good idea," she said, fighting back tears.

"What? Well, I'm a pretty good salesman when I want to be," he smiled. "Let me see you dive one more time, if you don't mind."

A huge smile rolled over Kelly's freckled face as she quickly raced to the locker room to change into her swimsuit. The coach gave her some instructions, and Kelly bounded up the stairs two at a time. She couldn't wait to get to the platform.

"Please, God, let this be a good dive." Again, she nailed the dive. A perpendicular entry. No splash. She popped to the surface like a cork, and couldn't believe her eyes when she looked around. There must have been a dozen people smiling and applauding. The coach gave her a big hug and an even bigger towel as she hopped out of the water.

"Do you mind if I talk with your parents, Kelly?" he asked. "Maybe they don't understand the extent of your talent and how much it means to you."

He was right. After a long talk with Kelly's parents, they agreed to allow her to try out for the team. They even began attending diving competitions and, before long, were screaming and cheering as loudly as the rest of the parents in the stands.

While Kelly never actually won any events, she was a steady top-five finisher. Her teammates could always count on her to make a "clutch" dive when they needed it most, and Kelly contributed to several overall meet victories, and even a league championship, for her high school.

Today, Kelly Ann is a mother of three active daughters, all of whom are involved with various sports. "They have a big advantage over me when I was their age—they're coordinated," she laughs. "If they express an interest in something, whether it's sports-related or not, I make sure they have an opportunity to go after it!

"It's amazing," she continued, "but after my parents said yes to diving, my overall relationship with them improved dramatically. They had showed confidence and trust in allowing me to take a little more control of my life. And I always respected them for changing their mind."

Kelly Ann said parents should allow their children to experience their potential, understand their limits, and enjoy their talents. Thanks, Kelly. I couldn't have said it better.

The Parable of the Talents

I like to refer to the parable of the talents in Matthew 25:14–30 when discussing spiritual gifts with parents. It's about a man who entrusted his three servants with safeguarding his money before departing on a trip. "To one he gave five talents of money, to another two talents, and to another one talent, each according to his ability. Then he went on his journey" (v. 15).

The servant who received five talents immediately doubled the investment through savvy trading. The servant who was given two talents also proved a shrewd money manager by parlaying the man's money. The servant who was left with one talent, however, decided to "play it safe" and bury the money.

When the man returned he was delighted to see that his two servants had demonstrated their investment ability by doubling his money. He was pretty tough on the third servant, however, calling him "wicked" and "lazy."

The moral? We can only profit by making full use of our God-given talents, our natural gifts. If we turn our back on our abilities, or bury them, we are only hurting ourselves and not honoring God. Help your children recognize their spiritual gifts—it can only benefit their futures and their self-esteem.

9

If You Really Want to Alienate Your Kids . . .
YOU SHOULD NEVER LET THEM GROW UP

There's no justice! Just as we're becoming proficient at parenting, some self-appointed expert psycho-babbler urges us to start "letting go." Fat chance! I was just beginning to like the little cookie cruncher. Sure he's twenty-six, but he's a late bloomer. Besides, he neeeeeeds me!

Listen, we've invested too many years to relinquish the reins just yet. Too many 1:00 A.M. feedings. Too many marginal report cards. Too many soccer games. Too may concerns about sniffles, the proper arch support, and finishing homework. Just too many around-the-clock worries to hang 'em up now. What do you think parenthood is—"temp work"?

Yes, that's exactly what God had in mind—a temporary assignment with incredibly awesome responsibilities. Unfortunately, some people see parenthood as a lifetime assignment with a "no cut/no trade" clause in their contract. Well-balanced couples are prepared to "bow out" of parenting—at least the hands-on portion of the job—by the time their children have reached adulthood. Hopefully, long before the age of twenty-six.

You have a right to be proud. You provided love, direction, limits, discipline, and enough Chicken McNuggets to gag an army. You helped your children to discover and unwrap their spiritual gifts and talents. You were supportive and honest. You allowed them to set their own boundaries as they proved faithful to your trust. You even opened your house to an assortment of stray dogs, frogs, snakes, and hamsters. Most important, you helped your children develop a value system that clearly differentiates between right and wrong, good and bad, morality and immorality.

After that much effort, "letting go" should be a joyous process —a positive affirmation that our children are arriving as mature, productive adults—proof positive that we've done a pretty good job as parents.

But not so fast. You're not done yet. There will be grandchildren to spoil, recipes to teach, tools to loan, and tons of technical assistance to provide. But the tough work, the really "heavy lifting" of parenting is finally behind you. For the rest of us, it's back to work.

CHILDREN ON LOAN FROM GOD

American poet Carl Sandburg once wrote, "A baby is God's opinion that the world should go on." But whose world? One minute we're two people "getting it together" as husband and wife, and the next we're driving home from the hospital with an eight-pound, nine-ounce, milk-guzzling, diaper-dirtying, sleep-busting wonder—all wrapped up in a fuzzy, pink blanket.

Don't panic. Let's keep parenthood in perspective. God gives us kids out of His faith, trust, and love for us. We're asked to do our best in training them up, and only our best. Our role—indeed, our commission from God—is to be earthly caretakers for His children.

Remember, too, that our kids are only "on loan" from God. They have been born for a higher purpose than merely mowing the lawn or making us proud when they score the winning goal—those are only parenting perks.

I WON'T LET THEM GO. . . . THE BIBLE TELLS ME SO
(Mother 'em, smother 'em, and choose all their clothes)

For the parent who has difficulty letting his child grow up, certain biblical passages (taken out of context) serve only to validate an already rigid and controlling style. They read in Colossians 3:20, for example, that children should be obedient to parents "in everything, for this pleases the Lord." They somehow manage to skip past the next verse: "Fathers, do not embitter your children, or they will become discouraged" (v. 21).

The rigid and controlling parent also identifies with (no, dearly loves) Ephesians 6:2: "Honor your father and mother." No doubt caps and T-shirts with those words would be megasellers at any platoon parenting convention. Seriously, there are some parents who use these, and other passages, as evidence that they are the dictators of their homes. They line up just slightly to the right of Atilla the Hun.

For me, few words capture the essence of parenthood with the clarity of Ephesians 6:4: "Fathers [Moms too], do not exasperate your children; instead, bring them up in the training and instruction of the Lord." The key phrase is "bring them up," which means to "nourish tenderly" when literally translated. The concept involves a three-prong approach that instructs us to bring up our children physically, mentally, and spiritually, using corrective discipline when required. Sometimes parents get so caught up in the rearing of children, they forget to "bring them up."

IS IT TOO EASY TO BECOME A PARENT?

I'm constantly amazed at how casual some rookies are about parenting. A friend from my police days once slapped me on the back and told me that he and his wife were expecting their first child. "Pretty nervous, I bet," I responded.

"No, not really," he said.

"Want to borrow a few good parenting books of mine? I have shelves full of them!"

"Thanks anyway, Greg, but we really just want to do our own thing. Wouldn't want to confuse ourselves with all those different opinions about how to raise kids."

He's got to be kidding, I thought. *He doesn't want to confuse himself?* And this from a guy who had failed his sergeant's exam after twelve solid weeks of study. Maybe ignorance is bliss.

Before becoming a police officer I had to take a written test followed by an oral examination . . . followed by a physical exam . . . followed by a polygraph test . . . followed by a physical agility test . . . followed by a psychological evaluation. Then I had to go to the academy for three months. All this so I could learn how to write tickets, take reports, and determine what jelly donuts to avoid because of the unsightly stains they left on blue uniforms.

In contrast, there's only one requirement to becoming a parent —a baby. Even a driver's license requires a written test followed by a rather simple driving test. I know it's simple because my brother passed it—after three attempts. But to have a baby? No experience or training necessary.

Prior to parenthood, what if prospective moms and dads had to pass an exam? The test would measure levels of commitment, such as how many years the applicant could endure Mutant Ninja Turtle reruns. No exam worth its weight in Twinkies would be complete without a take-home quiz. During this portion of the test the applicant would be assigned two loaner "quiz kids" for one week.

At the end of the exam period, the quiz kids would rate the applicant's parenting prowess. Questions might include

> Did they provide at least twelve hours of lively entertainment each day?
> Were they easily manipulated into allowing donuts for dinner?

If they indicated a thumbs down, sorry, no "kid permit" at this time —go to the end of the line, please—the applicant would then be required to take Remedial Parenting 101 (slow class) and could apply again in three months.

OK, I'm being sarcastic. But whatever happened to the good old days? The days when God hand-picked His parents with care— such as Abraham and Sarah. On second thought, I don't envy Abe having to make the long trek to the all-night Mini-Mart in Babylon for sardines and Pop Tarts because Sarah had a craving.

READ THE JOB DESCRIPTION FIRST

Prior to accepting any new position, most people want to become fully familiar with the job description. They naturally want to know exactly what the position entails and what's expected of them. Prospective parents should ask themselves the same thing, especially when you consider the length of the assignment. Questions such as

> Why do we really want this job?
> What are our kids going to need from us?
> Do we feel well suited for the position?
> Will we miss our free time together?
> Are we only looking for a change of pace?

Maybe we should start with something easier—say goldfish.

What if an employer ran the following classified ad? Can't you just hear the phones ringing off the walls with anxious applicants?

WORK AT HOME AND SPEND LOTS OF MONEY!

Small home business has immediate opening for motivated couple with strong communication skills. No experience necessary. Extremely long hours with no pay. Full benefits include brief moments of fulfillment between long periods of worry, frustration, and heartache. No insurance (strongly suggest you get some). Brothers and sisters optional. Dog not provided. Apply today. Call 1-800-FAT CHANCE.

It's too bad more couples don't read the fine print in the parenting job description before signing up. There would be fewer unhappy couples with troubled kids.

BECOMING CLEAR ON THE GOALS OF PARENTING

1 *First and foremost.* Help them grow to know God and to develop an interpersonal relationship with Jesus Christ. Don't forget your part as a role model and spiritual leader in your family.

2 *Instilling values.* Assist them in getting their own value system "off the ground" and into everyday practice. Hopefully, their value

system is a combination of the positive things they've learned from you—both through instruction and modeling—and their own belief system.

3 *Communicating social responsibility.* Help them prepare for responsible and mature relationships with both sexes. Assist in helping them to understand their sexual feelings and responsibilities in relationship to Christian standards, personal standards, and health standards. Allow them to make up their own minds about what is right and moral. If you give them an arbitrary no, they may rebel. If you're too easy, they'll take advantage.

4 *Recognizing and discussing change.* Help them to accept and understand their changing emotional and physical selves. Create an atmosphere that welcomes communication. Be prepared to initiate the conversation if necessary. Above all, keep it safe for them to bring up any topic.

5 *Preparing them for independence.* Help them to gain emotional independence from you and other adult authority figures in their life by allowing them to become more self-reliant.

6 *Helping them develop intellectually.* It's your responsibility as a parent to help them to improve their minds, as well as their batting averages or sewing skills. I've found that this is best started at an early age. Instead of watching so much TV, how about reading to them or doing word puzzles or crafts together.

7 *Teaching relationship.* Help them to understand the social and emotional roles between men and women, husbands and wives, parents and children. (Positive role modeling at home is very important.)

8 *Preparing them for the future.* Help them to become socially and financially independent. Counsel them in possible career paths long before they graduate from high school. That doesn't mean buying them medical books at age four, but keep an eye out for where their gifts and talents lie.

OBEDIENCE VS. INTIMIDATION

True, God does expect children to obey their parents. But there's a difference between willful obedience that helps a child grow mentally, emotionally, and spiritually and forced compliance accomplished through fear and intimidation.

I've known parents who were shocked when their children reached a particular stage at which they began to act up or rebel against their parents' authority through intimidation. "This isn't how we raised our kids," they might say with a shrug. Upon closer examination, however, the reasons for their children's alienation becomes clear. These are parents who have allowed "growth inhibitors" to sneak into their parenting styles. Feelings of minimization can severely inhibit your child's emotional growth and lead to rebelliousness. Let's take a look at some of the major growth inhibitors.

Ignoring or Discounting Your Child's Feelings

These parents might be heard to say, "Don't feel that way," or, "You shouldn't be taking this so hard." They have problems with acknowledging and honoring their child's feelings. Your children have every right to their feelings, whether you understand them or not. Furthermore, you should acknowledge and respect their feelings as you insist that others acknowledge and respect yours.

Feelings are never wrong. They are the personal property of the person having them. You may not agree, like, or understand the way your children feel, but you can't sweep their feelings away as if they don't exist. Your child's hurt feelings will mend faster if you are gentle, supportive, accepting, and loving.

Constant Disapproval and Conditional Approval

Did you ever work for a boss who constantly criticized your work? No matter how much effort you put into a report or a project, he always found something to criticize and complain about. Now think back to how you truly felt about your supervisor. If you are like most people, you probably felt minimized and unappreciated, and you resented his abuse of authority.

Children from emotionally withholding parents go through life feeling they never really measured up either. They never had the right friends. Their grades were never high enough. There was something wrong with any job they completed—like an overlooked, tiny patch of grass while mowing the lawn. These kids often develop a "defeatist" attitude. They start to think, *Why try so hard? Nothing will ever be good enough for my critical, withholding parent anyway.*

A Square Peg in a Round Hole

Parents who manipulate or pressure their children to become someone (or something) they're not are asking for instant alienation —for example, the little-league parent who pressures his son to play baseball, when all the boy really wants to do is join the chess club at school.

When in doubt, parents need to stop and ask themselves the following question: "How would *I* like being raised the way I'm raising him?" Again, this is where empathy can be a valuable tool for any parent.

Does this mean you always must give in to your children? Absolutely not. It simply means to become more considerate, observant, tolerant, and sensitive to their feelings. Try your best to include your children's personal boundaries (their wants, needs, likes, and dislikes) as part of your decision-making process.

THE DE-PARENTING PARADIGM

The amount of parental control and guidance required for children hinges on many factors and varies from child to child. However, the following two charts illustrate two vastly different parenting styles as regards the de-parenting paradigm.

In Chart A, notice how the amount of control and guidance (which is rather low in the early years) dramatically increases at about fourteen, a common age when a child begins to want more control over his life. Simultaneously, the parental line shoots up in an effort to restrain the child's ability to achieve greater independence.

In Chart B, I've diagrammed a more reasonable course for what I call the de-parenting paradigm. Control and guidance begins at a young age with moderate and appropriate levels and gradually increases into the teen years. You can see how there's room for a child to experience a "tapering-off" of parenting control as he reaches approximately fourteen years of age. This method encourages a teenager to become more independent and internally responsible.

All children mature at different rates—some sooner, some later. It's important that parents recognize and continually monitor

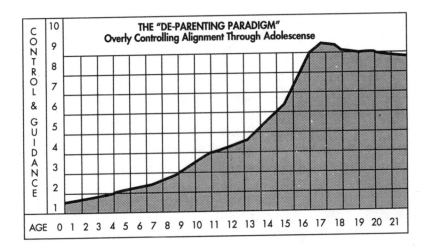

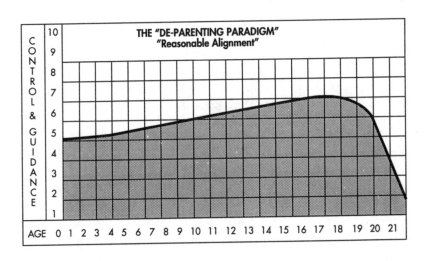

their child's level of maturation, then adjust their levels of guidance and control accordingly. Some parents can begin easing off the "authority pedal" when their child is thirteen or fourteen. Other children continue to need more structure until they are older.

MOTHER 'EM, OR NUDGE 'EM FROM THE NEST?

One of the most difficult parts of being a parent is allowing your children to test their little wings—especially for the first time. It's tough to shed that innate desire we all have to protect our kids, regardless of age, level of maturity, or need for independence.

How did you feel when you detached the training wheels from your child's bike for the first time? Apprehensive, right? You gave her a little nudge, and off she flew down the street. You sprinted to keep up in case she fell, but she quickly left you in the dust. Did you notice that giant grin on her face as she realized a measure of independence and accomplishment? Or was that at the sight of you standing in the middle of the street gasping for breath?

For most of us, flashes of maternal or paternal instincts surface frequently. For me, it happens whenever a boy shows up at my front door and wants to know if my eight-year-old daughter can come out to play. "No. She's moved to Fiji to become a missionary and live among the natives. Go away!"

It's natural to want to protect our kids from anything "bad" (like neighbor boys), potentially dangerous, or inappropriate for their innocent eyes. But there are also times when attempting to protect your kids can lead to problems. We've all heard the expression "overprotective parent." I plead guilty. I'm one of the original worry warts.

You're watching TV with your kids when something with sexual overtones pops on the screen. Do you take the time to explain why the material is inappropriate? No, you usually just snatch the remote control from their hot little hands and switch the channel to Monday Night Football.

Sure, you accomplished your mission, but perhaps a brief statement would have been in order. "You know, kids, I don't think we should spend family time watching shows without much value or meaning." This allows them to understand your rationale rather than fostering even more curiosity—you know, the "forbidden fruit" syndrome, when a kid wants to know exactly what it was you didn't want him to see. It also allows you to catch a few minutes of the Bears-Redskins game.

Here's another example of overprotecting in action. One day I told my wife that I never wanted my son to have any toy guns. It seemed a reasonable request. Many parents don't approve of toys that promote violence. And then it hit me. Every morning my son watched me go to work with a shiny, chrome revolver strapped to my side. Good thinking, huh? And I was a detective at the time.

Despite my early attempts at gun control, our son made firearms out of anything and everything. Bananas became Uzis and baby bottles turned into hand grenades. Diapers? They remained diapers. What could be more lethal? There are times when you have to face facts: you can't protect your children from everything, you can only do your best.

LET YOUR KIDS TEST-FLIGHT THEIR WINGS

Give your kids a chance to flap their wings and become airborne on their own. Without our support and encouragement, their ability to stay aloft could be diminished. They may even forget they have wings if they continually find themselves grounded securely under yours.

That doesn't mean letting your kid "crash and burn" on his first solo flight. You're the flight instructor, so check his progress periodically. Help him make any necessary midcourse adjustments.

A caller to my "talk show" once asked this question: "My twelve-year-old son thinks he is old enough to stay home by himself while my husband and I go out. I think twelve is too young, but my husband thinks it's all right."

She went on to list a few examples of her son's independence and trustworthiness, and I agreed that it was time to let him expand his boundaries. I suggested, however, that they not go out for a ten-course meal the first time—perhaps an hour or so, while calling home once to check on his progress. In this way, he could enjoy a sense of new-found independence, while feeling connected and protected at the same time.

Let your children experience their own limits and boundaries in increasing amounts as they mature and earn your trust. There will still be consequences for breaking your rules, but these will be more readily accepted and understood by a child who is becoming more responsible and moving toward adulthood.

NOT IN FRONT OF THE KIDS!

How many of us grew up believing our parents never argued. Most of the couples I see for marriage counseling fall into one of two categories: they never saw their parents argue, or their parents constantly argued.

I don't believe in hiding misunderstandings or disagreements from children. Kids (five and older) are able to deal with their parents' occasional conflicts without becoming crazed serial killers when they grow up. In fact, most experts agree that it's healthier for them to see some conflict and resolution between parents in order to have a realistic view of interpersonal relationships.

The important thing is to model a positive resolution through calm dialog—even if that dialog gets intense at times. Remember, resolution never means throwing things, name calling, holding your breath, pouting, or the ever-popular taking your ball and going home. Conflict resolution through calm dialog is an important lesson for your child to learn as he matures. It gives him permission to explore disagreement with you without fear that conflict will result in intolerable anger or withholding love.

Parents who hide conflict by retreating behind locked doors to vehemently argue are not doing themselves or their children any favors. After all, conflict is an inevitable part of any good relationship. As these children mature and form their own relationships, they won't know how to deal with their own conflicts. They might slam doors or angrily speed off in their car, thinking there must be something terribly wrong with them for feeling so angry with someone they like or love.

In the final analysis, all we can do is our best for God and His children. There's a lot to remember, but nobody ever said it was going to be easy. Before you know it, your kids will have grown up and have kids of their own. You'll be taking that long overdue cruise and chuckling to yourselves about revenge, sweet revenge.

10

If You Really Want to Alienate Your Kids . . .

KEEP TRYING TO BE THE "PERFECT PARENT"

You know you're having an off parenting day when . . .

- You can actually hear your words falling on deaf ears.
- Everything you say or do alienates your kids in at least ten different ways—and the day's still young.
- The neighbor kids are even starting to look good compared to your own little fire starters.
- Your kids would rather clean their rooms than do something with you.
- Your kids draw a picture of you being mauled by the family dog.

On those days when I've either misplaced my parenting tools, or when those I do find fail miserably, I gain solace from Luke 2:42.

As this story illustrates, even "world class," well-balanced parents can suffer temporary parenting setbacks.

Every year Mary and Joseph would cash in their "frequent caravan coupons," load up the donkey, and travel to Jerusalem for the traditional Feast of the Passover—not exactly a Club Med vacation, but an excellent travel package featuring outstanding shopping, food, and fellowship with family and friends.

Now a preteen, Jesus had always been included on these yearly excursions. Understandably responsible and mature for His age, He was allowed to mingle freely with other travelers in the vast caravan. Face it, it would be difficult putting boundaries on the Messiah.

Their stay in Jerusalem had proved a memorable one, but, as with any vacation, it was over much too soon. Before they knew it, the time had come to join the caravan and go home. Mary and Joseph had traveled an entire day before they noticed that something was missing—Jesus. Here they were, the hand-picked parents of God's only child, and He was lost—perfect! Talk about the original "Home Alone" concept.

Can't you just picture Mary? If she had been like most wives today, her hands would have been on her hips as she faced Joseph and nervously tapped one toe. "I thought you were watching the Messiah." To which he defensively responded, "Excuse me, dear. I thought *you* were watching the Messiah."

But this was no time for misplaced anger or finger pointing. They had a very special young man to find. They questioned everybody in the caravan, but nobody had seen Jesus. Panic set in. What if He had been injured en route? What if He had been kidnapped? What if they left Him behind? Mary looked at Joseph. Joseph looked at Mary. They both looked at the donkey. His ears immediately drooped: *We're going back to Jerusalem, just watch. Oh, my aching hooves.*

After running down one dead-end lead after another, the grief-stricken couple had just about given up all hope when they stumbled upon Christ: "After three days they found Him in the temple courts, sitting among the teachers, listening to them and asking them questions" (Luke 2:46).

Sure Mary and Joseph were upset (they had already shelled out to have His picture imprinted on local goat milk cartons), but there would be no discipline. They believed and trusted Him when He said, "Why were you searching for me? . . . Didn't you know I had to be in my Father's house?" (v. 49).

God realizes that no parent is perfect. We are all fallible—even the well-balanced parents Mary and Joseph. He shows us that just good enough is indeed enough. We should always remember to afford ourselves, our spouses, and our children the same margin for error and the same degree of compassion that God shows us.

I've often wondered, though, how our two most problematic parenting styles—platoon and pushover parent—would have handled the missing Jesus incident. If Mary and Joseph had been platoon parents, there would have been no incident at all. Jesus would have been on such a short leash, with such rigid limits and boundaries, that He would have been afraid to wander more than twenty feet away: "Jesus, You get back here this instant, Mister!"

If Mary and Joseph had been pushover parents, they wouldn't have been at all alarmed about His whereabouts: "We'll pick Him up the next time we pass through Jerusalem."

No Rest for the Weary

Nobody gets as pooped out as parents. Nobody. After a particularly lousy week of car pools, impossible deadlines at work, parent/teacher conferences, and Brownie Troop meetings, the last thing you need is to be awakened on Saturday morning by a familiar voice asking, "What should I use to get Super Glue out of the doggie's fur?" Please, not on Saturday morning!

Children know exactly how to get their way. Like half-crazed little animals, they stalk downwind of the docile, unsuspecting parent. They wait until you're on a long distance phone call or in the shower so that any nefarious activities are muffled by the sound of running water. They may observe you for hours waiting for just the right moment. Finally, they spring: "Can I have five dollars for the mall?" You hear yourself saying yes, and you still can't believe it.

Why do kids resort to trickery to get their way? Simple. It's because they hate to hear the word *no!* And for parents, the easiest way to avoid conflict is by saying yes. There's nothing to it, and the rewards are tremendous. The word yes is usually followed by "I love you, Mom" or "You're the greatest dad in the world."

Conversely, kids train their parents very early that the word *no* produces an assortment of undesirable emotions in our children—from temper tantrums to my personal favorite, "That's not faaaiiirrr!"

It's more fun to be Superdad—a genuine legend on the block, a hero among the neighbor kids, able to leap tall dog houses in a single bound. Is that really what you want?

While writing this chapter, I took a break to retrieve the newspaper from our soggy front lawn. As usual, I went straight to the "funnies." After reading "Peanuts," I was drawn to a strip called "Drabble" by Kevin Fagan. The cartoon showed a couple of kids playing outside as their parents watch from a living room window. The mother comments about how she wishes she didn't have to spoil their fun by telling them that it was time to come in. The father pontificates about how good parents should be willing to take responsibility for an unpopular decision and volunteers to deliver the bad news for his wife. But once outside he doesn't just tell the boys that it's time to come inside; he places the blame on their "mean ol' mom"!

Parenting should never be reduced to a popularity contest. If you are more concerned with how much your kids like you, rather than with what's best for them, you're destined for major issues of alienation.

Some parents are amazed to discover that their children continue to hold them in high esteem even after they've used the "no" word. Get this! Most kids will even (gulp) respect you for it. Imagine that.

So what will it be? The quick yes-fix or the more difficult, and unpopular, "no" course of action? Generally, I believe that the easiest, most expedient solution is usually the wrong way to go. There are no "parenting shortcuts."

A woman once came to my office after suffering a major parenting setback. She was dejected, convinced that she deserved to be the next Platoon Leader Poster Mom. It seemed that her eighteen-year-old daughter confided that she had felt fearful and nervous as a child over the prospects of ever disappointing her mom. Making matters worse were reports from her husband that her younger sister, nine, was having similar feelings of anxiety.

Before I could grant her enshrinement in the Platoon Parent Hall of Fame, however, I had to learn more—starting with Dad. This guy turned out to be the nicest, most easy-going dad any kid could "own." He was the ultimate pushover parent. Even "Leave It to Beaver" mom, June, would have looked like Freddy Kruger by comparison.

All of the unpleasant parenting decisions had fallen on her shoulders. She had set the limits and boundaries. She had to establish the consequences. She had to dispense the discipline. She was the one who said no. She had been forced into playing the role of villain—an unenviable, unpopular, and unfair position for any parent.

Next, I spoke with her children and discovered a completely different picture of Mom. True, they had been, and continued to be, concerned about disappointing their mother. And why not, since she was the only parent with expectations and boundaries? She was also the parent they came to when they were in trouble or needed help. They knew they would get an honest, accurate appraisal. Not simply a "Yes" or "That's nice, dear" answer.

When our sessions had concluded, Mom was feeling much better about herself. And Dad was scheduled for therapy. Exercising his "no" muscle was the first order of business.

TRY A LITTLE EMPATHY

No parenting tool box should be without empathy. My poor, abused Webster's Dictionary defines *empathy* as "the ability to share in another's emotions, thoughts or feelings." Or as that seventies folk song used to say, "walk a mile in my shoes." However, I feel Romans 12:15 captures the spirit of empathy best: "Rejoice with those who rejoice; mourn with those who mourn."

Unlike other gifts, such as music or sports, empathy is not a natural talent. It's a skill that children develop unconsciously by watching their empathetic moms, dads, and others. Show me a parent without empathy, and I'll show you a selfish parent. If empathy is not part of your parenting style, you are probably impeding the maturation of your children.

As a cop, I met my share of parents with severe empathy deficits. Regularly, I would be radioed to pick up a child or teenager for various violations, including shoplifting, curfew, and being drunk in public. Invariably, as I approached the front door with the troubled kid, I was greeted with "Could you please move your police car? I don't want the neighbors to see." Their first concern was clearly for themselves, not their child's problems. They didn't ask for advice or even referrals—all they wanted was my "black-and-white" moved.

If your parents were less than empathic, you may have to work a little harder to develop the skill. Start by not reacting to your kid's latest "screw up"; instead, try visiting his feelings. I'm not talking about a two-day layover—just long enough to nail down the probable motivating factors behind his actions. Next, ask yourself, "Can I help solve the problem, or am I exasperating an already emotionally charged issue?" An empathetic parent is one who attempts to think along with his child before acting.

Tune in to your kids. Anticipate their actions. My daughter once wandered over to my desk, and before she could utter a word I handed her a pair of scissors. "How did you know, Daddy?" I told her that sometimes I just know what she's thinking (which is going to drive her real crazy when she's a teenager). Of course, I never admitted to hearing her ask her mom for scissors thirty seconds earlier.

We can use empathy as a kind of radar detector to alert us to incoming kid problems. When your children are aware that you have empathy and are attempting to think along with them, they may be more comfortable coming to you with their sensitive personal issues and concerns.

The question is sometimes asked, "Should I intervene when I see a potential problem coming down?" There may be times when you feel strongly that your kid is on a troublesome path. If you need to intervene, avoid accusatory tones: "You know, honey, I was thinking about what I might do if I were in your place." Above all, open a meaningful dialog with your child.

Empathy in young children is a wonderful sight. If you have set a good example at home, it should begin to show up in your kids at about age four. I first noticed empathy in my son during an afternoon walk in the park. My daughter had just blasted past us on her roller blades when she suddenly stumbled and hit the ground with a thud. Some kids might have laughed (I know I was holding it back), but Matt immediately rushed over to his sister, patted her on the back, and asked if she was OK.

Family prayer time is another excellent way to communicate empathy to your children. Instead of praying in generalities, ask God for help in understanding your children. Your open prayers tell your kids how much you care about their feelings.

BALANCED PARENTS, BALANCED FAMILIES

Some parents place their children in the center of the universe. The result is a family that has gotten seriously out of balance. I counseled just such a family, where the marriage was on the verge of collapsing. The mom had put the needs of her children ahead of those of her husband. In fact, the kids' needs were ahead of everyone else's in every aspect of her life. When her husband came home from work, she had nothing left for him but leftovers—leftover time, leftover energy, leftover companionship, and leftover love.

This woman was raised in a home with four brothers and three sisters. Her father had toiled long hours at two different jobs. As you might have guessed, her mom placed the children at the center of the family unit as well. My client's husband, on the other hand, came from a well-balanced family where his mom and dad were together as a unit in the center, and the children revolved around them at equal distances. The kids were never far away emotionally, but not so close that they negatively impacted their parents' relationship. Nor did they ever get the feeling that they were individually more powerful than their parents' relationship.

The key is not losing sight of proper alignment in your family. This requires that your priorities remain in balance. Whenever a parent elevates one or more of the children to a position of too much emotional importance, there is always a risk of splitting the parenting team.

THE BEATITUDES OF PARENTING

How many among us practice half the things we preach to our children? Before instructing your children in how to keep their lives in order, I always suggest that parents refresh their memories of the Beatitudes in Matthew 5. This Scripture not only reminds us of God's instructions to us but also how the Beatitudes communicate the ground rules of balanced parenting.

Matthew 5:3   Blessed are the poor in spirit,
                        for theirs is the kingdom of heaven.

Parenting application Practice and live a life of humility. Don't be boastful or self-absorbed and then expect your children to be any different.

Matthew 5:4 Blessed are those who mourn,
for they will be comforted.

Parenting application Don't be too proud. Allow yourself to feel pain and express hurt and disappointment. This also allows your children the freedom to access their feelings and provides a safe place to express them.

Matthew 5:5 Blessed are the meek,
for they will inherit the earth.

Parenting application Don't parent through intimidation, control, and manipulation and then expect kindness and compassion from God.

Matthew 5:6 Blessed are those who hunger and thirst for righteousness, for they will be filled.

Parenting application If you don't study the Bible, pray with your children, and fellowship regularly, they will see you as a hypocrite when you expect more of *them* than *you* are willing to give.

Matthew 5:7 Blessed are the merciful,
for they will be shown mercy.

Parenting application Don't be afraid to apologize or ask your kids for forgiveness when necessary. Don't pretend to be the perfect parent. Understand, admit, and "own" your mistakes—just as you ask of them. Give second and even third chances whenever appropriate.

Matthew 5:8 Blessed are the pure in heart,
for they will see God.

Parenting application Don't say one thing and then do another. Say what you mean and mean what you say. Be honest about yourself in all situations.

	Be willing to admit and "own" your weaknesses as well as your strengths.
Matthew 5:9	Blessed are the peacemakers, for they will be called sons of God.
Parenting application	You have to approach all decision-making situations from a position of love, honesty, and fairness. Find resolution to conflict through dialog, truth, and grace.
Matthew 5:10	Blessed are those who are persecuted because of righteousness, for theirs is the kingdom of heaven.
Parenting application	Praise your children when they do well and provide them with boundaries and discipline when they are in need of guidance.

ERASERS, WHITE-OUT, AND SUPER GLUE

Whenever you're feeling shaky about your parenting style, remember that kids are resilient. They are uniquely capable of maneuvering through even the craziest of childhoods and still turn out great. You are going to make mistakes. We all do. Don't beat yourself up over them or abandon ship when the seas become turbulent.

The fact that you've picked up this book, or any other parenting book, tells me that you love your children enough to try to improve. Take a moment, relax, and pat yourself on the back. The world is full of parents who either don't realize they need to improve or wouldn't put forth the effort if they did.

SOME FINAL BELIEFS

I believe we have the power to make parenting a daily tortuous grind or immeasurable fun.

I believe we can worry ourselves to death if we allow ourselves to get too wrapped up in our everyday parenting mistakes.

I believe that laughter, especially that of a child, is one of the most precious commodities in the world—more precious than gold, or even beating your six-year-old in a game of Super Mario Brothers.

I believe parenthood is the most underrated, underappreciated, and underpaid profession in the world.

Finally, I believe that with hard work and perseverance, one day your kids will look back on their childhood with fondness. They will recognize that you did your very best. They might even express their appreciation for a job well done with a good old-fashioned bear hug and a quick word of thanks. If not, don't worry. I'm working on a new book: *Ten Ways Aging Parents Can Torment Their Adult Children.*

NOTES

Chapter 2
1. Evan Esar, *20,000 Quips and Quotes* (New York: Doubleday, 1968).

Chapter 3
2. N. Gregory Hamilton, *Self and Others* (Northvale, N.J.: Jason, 1990), 165.

Chapter 7
3. Lawrence Kutner, *Parent & Child: Getting Through to Each Other* (New York: William Morrow, 1991), 87–88.
4. "How Not to Bring Up a Bratty Child," *Redbook* magazine (October 1984), 29–31.

Chapter 8
5. Alan L. Berman and David A. Jobes, *Adolescent Suicide: Assessment and Intervention* (Washington, D.C.: American Psychological Assoc. Press, 1991), 40, 47, 54, 106, 109, 141, 212.

For more information regarding tapes, speaking engagements, or counseling, write or call:

Dr. Greg Cynaumon
American Pychological Institute
115 Chaparral Court # 102
Anaheim Hills, CA 92802
(714) 283-9224

Moody Press, a ministry of the Moody Bible Institute,
is designed for education, evangelization, and edification.
If we may assist you in knowing more about Christ
and the Christian life, please write us without obligation:
Moody Press, c/o MLM, Chicago, Illinois 60610.